CW00545289

SOUTHAMPTON
in the 1980s

Ten Years that Changed a City

GARTH GROOMBRIDGE

AMBERLEY

First published 2014

Amberley Publishing
The Hill, Stroud
Gloucestershire, GL5 4EP

www.amberley-books.com

Copyright © Garth Groombridge, 2014

The right of Garth Groombridge to be identified as the Author
of this work has been asserted in accordance with the
Copyrights, Designs and Patents Act 1988.

All rights reserved. No part of this book may be reprinted
or reproduced or utilised in any form or by any electronic,
mechanical or other means, now known or hereafter invented,
including photocopying and recording, or in any information
storage or retrieval system, without the permission in writing
from the Publishers.

British Library Cataloguing in Publication Data.
A catalogue record for this book is available from the British Library.

ISBN 978 1 4456 4182 9 (print)
ISBN 978 1 4456 4192 8 (ebook)

Typesetting and Origination by Amberley Publishing.
Printed in the UK.

Contents

Introduction

Moving to Southampton in 1985 from Middlesex (now West London), the initial impression I had was of a rather dull, if at times perhaps rather eccentric, provincial town, rather than a city. War and town planners had obliterated large chunks of the city's past, while, as various civic plans came and went, it was seemingly hesitant and unsure about its future. Like so many British towns and cities, it had suffered the blight of 1950s/1960s modernism, resulting in haphazard, uncoordinated and poor planning.

An example of the latter was the disappearance, in July 1987, of the Hants & Dorset Bus terminus (which had originally opened in 1933) between Windsor Terrace and Portland Terrace. Marlands now occupies this site. Twenty-five years later, despite promises, the city still awaits a proper, centralised bus terminus like Portsmouth still has at the Hard, or Winchester (for now, at least) in Broadway. At the same time, the 1938 coach station in Bedford Place (originally extending into Grosvenor Square) was also closed, to be replaced by several huge, rather joyless office blocks, while a 'temporary' coach station existed for the next decade on the derelict Pirelli site, directly opposite the town walls and the 'Forty Steps'. Throughout the 1990s, late at night, it was a grim and bewildering introduction for visitors – dark, desolate and lifeless, with the prospect of having to find one's own way through the backstreets of Simnel Street into Bugle Street, or (if lucky) into Above Bar Street. It only relocated to its present (still not ideal) site between the Asda store and Toys 'R' Us in 1999.

During this period, the city lost its zoo, opened in 1961 and closed in 1985, the site now being the Hawthorns Urban Wildlife Centre in Cemetery Road, and the much-loved Bird Aviary in East Park, dating from the 1930s, and disappeared a bit later, in the early 1990s. Perhaps one of the most controversial changes during this time was the closure of the Ice Rink Sportsdrome complex in Archers Road by the then owners Top Rank in 1988, not just for the mean and underhanded way it was done (Rank had been scheming to demolish and sell the site for housing for some considerable time), but the broken promises made by the city council and others that a replacement facility would be built. Instead, and over twenty-five years later, this still rankles many older Sotonians – the nearest ice rinks are Basingstoke or Gosport. In 2012, yet another proposal for a new ice rink at St Mary's fell through.

More important for this period were the schemes that were being proposed. Some came to fruition, but were not always successful, or quite what had been envisaged, and at least some of these are portrayed in the pictures and text in this book. Other schemes – perhaps the classic examples are the original 1985 proposals, since then seemingly revised every decade, for Royal Pier and Mayflower Park – still await development in 2014. The Royal Pier especially is a disgrace – a burnt-out, overgrown, derelict thirty-year-plus eyesore – while Mayflower Park is dull and rather dreary, an opportunity that continues to be unfulfilled.

Almost forgotten now, however, are two of my favourites from the 1980s; first, the intriguing, but perhaps ultimately under-ambitious, 1987 'Metro 2000' (or 'People Mover') proposals. At the time, I recollect the publicity video, but just recently I found some rather awful project drawings on the internet, sadly (as is often the case with such illustrations) completely failing to give a true picture of either the appearance or visual impact of the scheme in question. This was to be a 2.5-mile circular monorail linking the central railway station (the then coach station and the central baths) – Town Quay and the ferries (Ocean Village) – Debenhams (where direct access to the first-floor level of the store was planned) – then across Hoglands and Houndwell Parks to Vincent's Walk (where the local city buses still congregate) – then onto the Civic Centre, and back to the central station. Fascinating as the scheme was, it had a number of flaws – not least the potential cost (even a conventional tramway system similar to Croydon or Manchester would probably have been cheaper), but also the need for Parliament to revoke various by-laws needed to construct across the public parks. Although there *was* some talk of later extending the system beyond the confines of the city centre, the failure to include links, say, north to the University campus, or west to Shirley and east to the suburbs of Woolston or Bitterne, meant the idea was too localised. While in retrospect it might have become a tourist attraction, for most locals it was probably quicker to walk!

A year later, in February 1988, the city council proposed a much more interesting redevelopment, and one which, perhaps even now, might have transformed the area around Upper Above Bar Street and the Civic Centre. In two coloured brochures entitled *Northern Above Bar Redevelopment*, the proposal was to close off and pedestrianise Above Bar Street from New Road to Commercial Road, with, from Gibbs Road onwards, what would then become a two-level shopping mall under a 'lofty glazed roof'. This would extend across a new first-floor public area to be known as 'Guildhall Court' (slightly smaller than the existing Guildhall Square), from where more steps, escalators and elevators would lead onto West Marlands and a elegant piazza, with trees and a fountain in front of the Guildhall itself. While both Tyrrell & Green and C&A would have been incorporated into the new mall (the former actually enlarging their premises by extending their frontage forward and having access at both ground and first-floor level), the 'Plummers and Cannon Cinema blocks' (now Solent University's Sir James Matthews Building and the KFC to Subway block) were to be demolished and completely rebuilt, with another entrance to the first-floor level on the Civic Centre Road corner (actually where KFC is now). Within this new complex were to be 450,000 square feet (4,180 square metres) of small shops or commercial units on two levels, and 800-capacity multi-storey car parks, with the vehicle access from Park Walk and a new service road and ramp running in from opposite Watts Park. Only the parade of existing shops to the extreme north and south of Tyrrell & Greens would have survived, although their frontage would have now been paved and pedestrianised. This was both exciting and interesting, especially when viewed within the general context of other ongoing development proposals, such as the Bargate Centre, then still being envisage to extend across Queensway to Debenhams, and the Marlands, which was being planned to connect to a 'shopping and business uses, transport and parking facilities, and a residential area, plus a multi-purpose "town arena"' in the Western Esplanade area. Again, we are still waiting for that last facility. Yet another unfulfilled project was the redevelopment of the Woolworths site (what are now the three-level TK Maxx and BUYology stores), where another 'development comprising thirty-three smaller shops arranged in an attractive covered mall part of which will be built over the bus terminus at Vincents Walk … [and] also provide covered links into Marks and Spencer and British Home Stores [now Primark and BHS], as part of a wholly integrated shopping centre.' Like the Above Bar Street scheme, that also came to nothing.

The 1980s saw the beginnings of the transformation of Southampton into the modern (if, at times, still rather chaotic) city it now is, starting with Ocean Village and Town Quay, continuing with the Bargate Centre and Marlands and, finally, in the late 1990s, culminating in WestQuay. I have included them all because they are crucial to the ongoing changes Southampton – whether good, bad or somewhere in between.

Ocean Village, Canute Road & Terminus Terrace

The history of Southampton as a modern port starts here, with the construction of the 16-acre Outer Dock (now the Ocean Village Marina) in August 1842, with the closed, non-tidal Inner Dock following in 1851. Further development and dry docks and berths followed right up until the First World War: The Empress Dock in 1890; Trafalgar Dry Dock in 1905; Ocean Dock, originally called the White Star Dock, in 1911 (where the RMS *Titanic* sailed from a year later). The inter-war years saw the filling-in of Western Bay, from the base of the old medieval town walls eventually all the way to Redbridge, after which the fortunes of the Old, or Eastern, Docks ebbed and flowed. By 1963, the Inner Dock had been filled in, becoming a car park for the Townsend Thoresen roll-on roll-off continental ferry, while in 1967 the Outer Dock was renamed the Princess Alexandra Dock. By 1984, however, while Ocean Dock continued being used by Cunard (and still is today), the cross-Channel ferry services were gradually pulling out, and so new ambitious plans were afoot to develop the entire 75-acre site into what was already being called 'Ocean Village'.

This and next page: These images are just three of a number of external photographs of the initial phase Canute's Pavilion, eventually constructed in two phases on the footprint of the former 'Shed No. 9' on the north side (formerly berths 9, 8 and 7) of the old Outer Dock, henceforth referred to as the 'Ocean Village Marina'. The first phase opened in July 1986, incorporating the red-brick 1920s intercontinental ticket office as its main entrance; with the second phase, seen in the pictures opposite, extending in stages along the quay towards the new Royal Southampton Yacht Club building (itself opened 1987). Within a short time, the foreground of photograph (*above right*) was occupied by the additional striped, brick extension seen in the photograph below, very soon to be rented out to Delta Belle. The promotional brochure announced that the shops in the two-storey mall traded from 10.30 a.m. until 8 p.m., but 'the wine bars and restaurants stay open a lot later', and 'All under one roof, seven days a week.'

These are two of three pictures I took of the interior of Canute's Pavilion – naturally now I wish I had taken more. Unlike the vivid reds, yellows and blues of the exterior, here the predominate colour was white, and it was essentially a very functional, almost industrial, two-storey design. In retrospect, it is quite modest in scale even compared to the Bargate Centre, and certainly to WestQuay, built fifteen years later. One website (chronicling the history of the Harbour Lights cinema) was rather dismissive of the low-brow nature of the retail businesses and entertainments here, saying it was comprised of 'trinket shops, fast-food outlets, theme bars and assorted life-sized fibre-glass sea creatures suspended from the ceiling'. Be that as it may, it was, for just over a decade, a popular place for cheap and cheerful food, ice-cream, live entertainment (music, dance troupes, people in funny costumes), a waterfront promenade (which Southampton still lacks), and a selection of interesting and eclectic shops and costermonger stalls. For a number of years after it opened, I remember there was a detailed project model of how the finished Ocean Village would eventually look, displayed under a glass case. Where is that model now, I wonder? The original brochure illustration for the project bears almost no resemblance to what we have today.

The only clue left to connect this location to that of the picture of Canute's Pavilion are the railway tracks, still embedded into the brick paving. Viewed here *c.* 2009, almost everything of the 1986/87 'first phase' Ocean Village, on the north side of the old Outer Dock, has vanished. This is now Admiral's Quay. Originally, as envisaged by then developer Wilson Bowden, there were to be ten ground-floor restaurants and bars, and eight blocks of apartments, named in the original sales brochure as Rainbow Court (nearest Channel Way), Endeavour Court (facing Canute Road), Velsheda Court and Shamrock Court. Apparently the names are now different. Facing the north-west side of the marina, but not built, were Yankee Court, Whirlwind Court and Britannia Court. It would appear that only the smaller Ranger Court, facing Ocean Way, has retained its original designated name. Unfortunately, even by February 2006, the scheme was in trouble and, in 2007, the developer went into administration and Barratt Homes acquired the site, their commercial arm having purchased the Wilson Bowden portfolio for £2.2 billion. Only half the project had actually been built, and only two restaurants were open, Banana Wharf and Pitcher & Piano. In 2011, having failed to either recommence work or sell it to another developer, Barrett Homes sold the site to the Southampton-based Allied Developments (owned by Charles Dunstone, the co-founder of TalkTalk and the Carphone Warehouse group) for £5.7 million. Their new architects, HGP, who designed Portsmouth's Spinnaker Tower, drew up a new £74-million proposal for nearly 300 new homes in three more towers (the tallest being 28 storeys, 260 feet or 79.2 metres), together with up to eight new restaurants. However, with the 2012 price tag of between £160,000 and £700,000 for the penthouse duplexes, and custom-designed apartments at £1 million, these are obviously not for ordinary Sotonians.

With the demolition of Canute's Pavilion in 2008, only the old 1920s intercontinental passenger ticket office survived, standing in isolation initially as the Wilson Bowden sales office. From 2009 until 2012, it enjoyed a brief purposeful reincarnation as the Mocha Marina Coffee Shop, an independent company set up by two female entrepreneurs. They shared the premises with a fitness studio and the Vikki Pink beauty parlour; the latter has since moved to new premises in the High Street. Unfortunately, with yet another broken promise, and despite last-ditch attempts to have the old building listed with English Heritage, it too was demolished in September 2012, the site having since disappeared beneath the foundations of the massive new 28-storey tower block, which at the time of writing (2014) is still under construction. However, by then, another memorable Ocean Village icon had also vanished – the bright, red Calshot Spit Lightship (LV78), built in 1914 by J. I. Thorneycroft, decommissioned in 1978 (*see photograph, taken c. 1990, reproduced on back cover.*) Having been relocated in front of the main 'Ticket Office' entrance to Canute's Pavilion from 1988 until 2008, it was then moved to Trafalgar Dock, where six years on, it still waits public view.

This is the transformed view of Admiral's Quay in 2014, following the Allied Developments/ HGP proposals, as seen across the marina from the quayside in front of Atlantic Close. A now completely dwarfed Enterprise House can be seen on the left, with (moving right) the upper storeys and roofline of Dart House (also known as Maritime Chambers), built in 1899 in yellow brick. The front pediment facing Canute Road has the initials London & South Western Railway (LSWR). For much of its early life, it was used by various shipping companies, including Cunard White Star Lines and Dart Container Line, from which it got its current name. Along the rear upper storey in the late 1980s was the inscription (since completely obliterated), 'Furness Withy Agency – Serving North & South America – The Middle & Far East'. Dart was then being within the Furness Withy group. To the right of that is the distinctive red brick and Dutch gables of Canute Chambers, built in 1893 for the American Line, occupied by the White Star Shipping Co. from 1907 to 1931. Looming up behind these more historic buildings are the rather bland student accommodation blocks, which we will see again close-up in Canute Road. The old Canute's Pavilion site, and what would have been Yankee Court, Whirlwind Court and Britannia Court in the Wilson Bowden plan, is now instead these towering apartment blocks. At the time of writing, the taller western (No. 1) building is not yet complete, with the glass cladding only just nearing the upper floors. When finished, this will be the tallest building in Southampton, and another 'landmark' building in the city council's current idiom. The centre (No. 2) building next to it is a 'mere' sixteen storeys, connected to its giant neighbour by an elevated terrace, with (so the blurb tells us) 'provision for up to eight restaurants and seating spilling out onto the promenade', and 'a public space on a human scale'.

A *c*. 1986 view of what is now Enterprise House, Ocean Village, following its extensive refurbishment from the last surviving Victorian warehouse into its new usage as a five-storey commercial office space, here seemingly standing in splendid isolation in a bleak landscape. It was originally just one of several warehouses located on the north side (berths 10, 11 and 12) of the closed, non-tidal, Inner Dock (opened in 1851, deepened and the entrance widened by 1859). For many years, it was dwarfed by a much larger warehouse, which was eventually destroyed by bombs in November 1940. The Inner Dock dealt mostly with the import of timber, grain and fruit, but all the warehouses on the north side were marked as being 'grain' warehouses on the 1910 Ordnance Survey, and again in 1933. In 1963, the entire Inner Dock (berths 10–18) was filled in, at first to be used as the car park for the cross-channel Townsend Thoresen roll on/roll off ferries, based on the west side of the Outer Dock (where the Harbour Lights Cinema is located now). Later it was planned as the Ocean Village development from 1986 onward, now occupied by Tagus House, the Meridian, Prospect and Grove Houses block, and Savannah House, with their respective surface car parks and the raised water feature. Thirty years later, and, with the demolition of the former continental booking office façade in 2012, the old Victorian warehouse is now the sole surviving link to the past; its surface car park, seen here, is now landscaped with low hedges. Savannah House (which, when it opened in 1986/87, was occupied by the accountants PricewaterhouseCoopers) now blocks the left-side view. The five-screen multiplex, Cineworld Cinemas now blocks the open view to the right, with the extremely attractive multi-storey Ocean car park situated beyond that.

The then ABC Cannon Cinema complex nearing completion, viewed across the Mermaid Way car park from Ocean Way, with Enterprise House on the left, *c.* 1988/89. Officially No. 4 Ocean Way, it opened in July 1989 with five auditoriums and a total of 1,650 seats. However, by 1992, it was owned by MGM, and since then its name has changed to Virgin, UGC, and now Cineworld. Outwardly it looks little different today, and the Egyptian-like temple is not unattractive – certainly visually better then the awful 'metal box' that is the Odeon Leisureworld in West Quay Road.

In a completely different architectural style, and designed by architects Burrell Foley Fisher at the cost of £1.5 million, the Harbour Lights Cinema, begun in 1993 and opened in 1995, was originally as a joint venture between Southampton City Council and the British Film Institute. It specialises in classical, foreign, art house and repertory films, as well as mainstream commercial pictures. Facing the marina, it occupies the site of the mid-1960s Townsend Thoresen roll-on/roll-off continental ferry terminal, which ceased operation in 1984, the building originally being earmarked for the new maritime museum. Instead it was demolished, and the new cinema, being designated a regional film theatre heritage project, was a compromise. Unfortunately, by 1999, it was in financial trouble, briefly closing, to reopen again under the Picturehouse Cinemas brand (founded in 1989, also known as City Screen Ltd). In 2012, Cineworld acquired all the Picturehouse cinemas for £47.3 million, but have promised (so far) to keep the more niche Harbour Lights. The inset photograph was taken in 1995, before the café bar terrace was built. The Southampton (later National) Oceanography Centre building (part of the University of Southampton, itself opened in 1996) can be seen in the background. Since 2011, an attractive Linden Homes apartment block now occupies the derelict space beyond the parked cars.

Comparing these two pictures (*c.* 1988 and 2014) of Bank House, at the Canute Road/Ocean Way entrance to Ocean Village, viewed from Canute Road, perhaps perfectly illustrates the colossal changes to this area in less than thirty years. In the second picture, the two-storey Canute Pavilion has gone and the former bank building is now completely dwarfed by Admiral's Quay, the new buildings, still under construction, that have replaced it. Built in 1896, the two-storey red-brick Bank House was originally the Grant & Maddison's Union Bank, itself an 1888 amalgamation of Maddison, Atherley & Co (est. 1869) of Southampton, and Grant, Gillman and Long (est. 1781) of Portsmouth. They had branches in Southampton, Portsmouth, Gosport and later Lyndhurst, and were taken over by Lloyds in 1903. In 2014, it is currently occupied by the high-class property firm Chesterton Humberts ('since 1805', it likes to proclaim). To its rear, in the later picture, is the three- and four-storey Ranger Court (part of the original Wilson Bowden plan), comprising of apartments with a Tesco Express on the ground floor. From the mid-nineteenth century until the 1980s, there was also a police lodge next to Bank House, which was demolished when the road was widened. Also of interest, shown on the 1910 Ordnance Survey and seemingly located where the car park behind Ranger Court is now, is the sixteenth-century 'site of the Admiralty Gallows'.

Canute Road & Terminus Terrace

Canute Road formerly connected 'the Beach' (now Platform Road) with Crosshouse and the Itchen ferry, and is named after Cnut the Great (*c*. 995–1035), the Danish-born King of Denmark, England and Norway, perhaps best remembered for the story commemorated by the Victorian plaque still seen on the wall of what was the Canute Castle Hotel (No. 13 Canute Road): 'Near this spot 1028 AD Canute reproved his courtiers.' The story of Canute failing to stop the tide is probably apocryphal, and although local legend claims it took place at 'Canute Point', roughly where the Victorian docks were built, there is at least one alternative location, that of Thorney Island (what is now Westminster), where Cnut was known to have a royal palace.

Overleaf: Seen here in the late 1980s, from left to right are Nos 3–6 Canute Road, part of the delightful eclectic parade between St Lawrence Road and Royal Crescent Road, built 1850–52. Nos 2–3 (the former out of the picture) was once a chemist, and at the time of this photograph was a shipping agent's, while No. 4 was then the Disability Resources Centre. No. 5 was built 1852 as the Ship Hotel or Ship Tavern, and the words 'London & Dublin – Stout House' can been be seen in black bricks on the façade. It ceased to be a public house in 1933, after which it was listed as 'Refreshment Rooms', eventually becoming the Canute Café, as seen here. At the time of writing it is a steakhouse called the 'Steak & Spice', but by July 2014 it was closed and boarded up. No. 6 was originally Miller's Clothier's, with (from 1861) the Sailors' Home at Nos 7–8, and J. R. Stebbing, the optician and maker of nautical instruments, located at No. 9. A post-war glass-fronted building, with two storeys above a basement, can be seen occupying what had been Nos 7–9, housing the popular Southampton Dockworkers' Social Club, although architecturally it made no concession to the Victorian buildings on either side. It became redundant when Associated British Ports replaced their workforce with contractors. It was eventually demolished and the site was tastefully redeveloped by Orchard Homes in 2005/06 as a very attractive four-storey apartment block, in what I call the European style, Nos 1–34 Canute Apartments. Canute Road has been a conservation area since 1986.

No. 1 Canute Road (built 1850, seen above *c.* 1986) completes what has survived of this mid-Victorian parade extending into St Lawrence Road, which itself had originally joined Canute Road with the now vanished Bridge Road – before the new Central Bridge was constructed and opened in July 1882. On the 1881 Ordnance Survey, the previous early Victorian Goods Shed is shown abutting Canute Road, approximately where Atlantis Court is now. No. 1 Canute Road was known as the New York Hotel until 1874 (a early engraving of the 'new' docks, presumably from the 1850s, as it shows only buildings on the north side of Canute Road, has a giant American flag flying from the roof), after which it became the London & Southwest Steam Packet offices. In 1897, it became known as Southwest Chambers and, like its immediate neighbours, continued to house various hauliers, freight companies and shipping agencies for the next eight decades. Until the Second World War, a second parade of Victorian buildings extended down St Lawrence Road on the right, including No. 7, the Providence Hotel, listed as such in *Kelly's Street Directory* from 1907 to 1940. The plain three-storey brick building seen here is post-war, probably dating from the 1950s or 1960s.

This image was captured at the same time as the previous image, but now looking along St Lawrence Road from Canute Road at the former Victorian Railway Goods Shed. It was built in 1882 in the Gothic style, and most sources say designed by Sir William Tite (1798–1873), a prolific railway buildings architect who also designed Terminus Station. However, given when Sir William died, the design must have predated the actual construction by more than a decade. Although regarded as an outstanding example of late-Victorian railway architecture, it ceased handing goods or parcels in 1967 and the tracks were all taken up by 1970, with the exception of the single track across Canute Road into the docks. It was Grade II listed in 1981. At the time of this photograph it was being used as Pickfords homepack container store. Somewhat to my surprise, I found a connection between Pickfords (which was established in the seventeenth century, making it one of the UK's oldest companies) and British Railways. In 1920, Pickfords was sold to Hayes Wharf Co., which, in turn, was taken over by four railway companies in 1934. When the railway companies were nationalised in 1947, the Pickfords arm became part of British Road Services, which, in 1969, became the National Freight Corporation. Later still in 1982, with privatisation seemingly resulting in an employee buyout, it was renamed the National Freight Consortium.

St Lawrence Road, as seen in 2014 and in 2007, is essentially now the private property of Solent University with its own metal security gate. The old Grade II listed Victorian goods shed is now only visible from Royal Crescent Road, its spacious interior used for student car parking, but this view is now completely dominated by disappointingly bland blocks of student accommodation of between five and eight storeys. Atlantis Court faces onto Canute Road, between St Lawrence Road, and the railway track, with Drake Court on the left. No. 1 Canute Road is now Lettings Direct, yet another property agent's, the same as the Canute Castle Hotel, at the other end of this parade, which has been there for the last fifteen years. Both specialise in properties within Ocean Village.

This and next page: On both the 1897 and 1910 Ordnance Survey, there are as many as six railway lines crossing Canute Road here. By 1972, there were two; now there is only one, mostly used to transport bulk wagons of motor cars destined for export, or the passengers (sometimes in Pullman carriages) to the Ocean Dock and Cunard's Queen Elizabeth II passenger terminal. From here the line crosses Maritime Way, runs parallel to Central Road, then runs down Ocean Road and finally to Test Road, with metal gates and stop signals either side. Only in 1981 were these automatic red, flashing lights installed, to replace the tradition method of men with red flags designated to stop the traffic for the duration of the train crossing Canute Road. The two circular brick and stone piers on the south side of Canute Road are located between the quite delightful single-storey 1907 'Wilts & Dorset Bank' building and the 1990s Charter House. They are listed, while two more identical piers also survive, now situated between the old National Westminster Bank, Chambers and Wight House, where the other railway tracks once crossed the road, going towards the old Outer and Inner Docks and Empress Dock. In 1999, East Anglia Railways proposed a rail link to run from the main junction near the St Mary's Stadium down to the waterfront, a project codenamed as 'T14'. Sadly, despite support by Southampton City Council (who reputedly safeguarded the land in anticipation), the idea – like so many good ideas for reinvigorating the maritime area of the city – fell almost at the first hurdle. When I read of this project, I thought that the old Union Castle House (built 1857 and used as the offices of the Union Line from 1892) would have made an ideal railway station building – it has the perfect rather grand façade. At that time it was still offices, but has since (rather bizarrely) been converted into apartments. Yet another opportunity lost.

The splendid Grade II listed South Western House, viewed from Platform Road, with Canute Road on the right, Queen's Park and Terminus Terrace on the left, taken sometime in the late 1980s, when it was still occupied by Cunard and the BBC. Designed by John Norton in the French Renaissance style, it was opened (still incomplete) in 1867 as The Imperial Hotel, before being taken over by the London & South Western Railway in 1871. The name was changed the following year to the South Western Hotel. Basically L-shaped, it extended in one direction along Canute Road, and along Terminus Terrace in the other direction (in 1927 the later, rather more austere, extension was constructed). At one time it was possible to see right through the ground floor to the platforms of Terminus station immediately behind. As a hotel in its Edwardian heyday, it saw tycoons, movie stars and royalty pass through its doors, as well as the first-class passengers about to embark on the ill-fated maiden voyage of the *Titanic* in 1912. Having been abruptly closed in August 1940, it was never to reopen again. Instead it became the naval base HMS *Shrapnel* and, in July 1942, the headquarters for the wartime Military Movement Control. In the immediate post-war period, it served as area headquarters for the National Service, offices for various government departments and British Rail. In the 1960s, it was occupied by BBC South (from 1961) and the Cunard Line. The former moved out to their own purpose-built headquarters in Havelock Road in 1991, the latter to Richmond House in 1997, before relocating again to Carnival House in West Quay Road in 2009. The property was then acquired in 1998 by Berkeley Homes, and now houses eighty-six flats. The Grand Café restaurant and bar is located in the former Wedgewood Ballroom.

Until the middle of the nineteenth century, Queen's Park, the eastern end, which can been seen on the left, was called Porter's Mead or Meadow, and was Lammas, or common land. It is still owned by Queen's College, Oxford, hence its new name after being leased, originally by the town council (now Southampton City Council), to become a public park. Even in 1985, the city planning department were proposing 'improvements to Platform Road and the elimination of one-way traffic circulation ... [to] enable the Park to be integrated more closely with the Oxford Street area'. Nearly thirty years later, in 2013/14, this is only just taking place.

Two 1980s views of the former Terminus Terrace railway station, the first taken in November 1985 of the attractive Italianate front façade, as seen from the already closed-off Oxford Street, with the north side of the still imposing Royal Mail Steam Packet Co. building on the right (it is still called Royal Mail House), and the London Hotel public house on the left. Built in 1839 and operational from 1840, it was designed by Sir William Tite, and was the original Southampton railway station before Southampton West (now Southampton Central) opened in Blechynden Terrace. It changed its name a number of times: Southampton Docks in 1859; Southampton Town & Docks in 1896; Southampton Town for the Docks in 1912; and finally Southampton Terminus in 1923. Not long after, it also acquired the splendid glass canopy over the platforms at the rear in 1927, linking the station to South Western House. Seen here in the second photograph (probably taken around 1988), thankfully this too has survived, despite bomb damage during the Second World War, although where the platforms once were is now only a car park. In 1987, it was refurbished and has had a new life as a restaurant, night club and casino under various names like Jeeves, Curzon, Stanley, and later Mint Casino. Currently, in 2014, it is the Genting Casino.

Another view, taken at the same time as the first picture above (November 1985), this time from the then still semi-derelict front of the former Terminus Station, looking north along Terminus Terrace. Note the wooden hoarding on the left and outgrowth of shrubs on the right, which appear in the previous picture. It is possible to read the inscription 'Postal Telegraphs' on the building being demolished in the middle foreground, which was built in the 1870s as a postal and telegraph office. However, from 1988 onwards, all of this had been developed as Captain's Place – pleasant, but again, rather bland housing. At one time in the nineteenth century, on the opposite side of Terminus Terrace from Oxford Street to what is now Bernard Street, there used to be numerous hotels, but they fell into decay from the 1940s, and were demolished by the mid-1980s. The 1975 *Kelly's Street Directory* gives a hint at what was here, listing, from Oxford Street northwards: No. 2 London Hotel, No. 3 Davis Hotel, Nos 4–5 William Hill turf agents, Nos 8–11 residential, No. 12 tobacconist, Nos 13–14 Parkers Hotel. Now, only the 1907 green, tiled Art Nouveau-style London Hotel is still there, a gay pub with cabaret and karaoke nights. What had once been the Railway Hotel next door has now been converted to residential use. In the 1985 photograph there is just fenced off, empty space, until Nos 113–14 on the corner of Terminus Terrace. Built in 1853, over the years, in addition to being known as Parker's Hotel, it has been called Captain's Corner, the Tut and Shive, and more recently the Court Jester. Since 2013, it has been called Captain's Place, a hotel, bar and restaurant. In 2014, the glass-fronted Nos 4–12 Terminus Terrace is now College Keep, an adult mental health unit for the NHS.

John Street, taken in November 1985 at the same time as the Terminus Terrace photograph (*above*), looking towards the rear of properties in Oxford Street. The taller red-brick building is the rear of Nos 35/36, Oxford House, the groundfloor of which is now 'Simon's at Oxfords', a wine bar and restaurant. It is an older, probably early nineteenth-century building with a 1920s/30s Edwardian-era street façade. In the 1975 *Kelly's Directory*, it was listed as the Naval & Nursing Outfitters and Tailors. It is now 'Oxford's Bar and Restaurant'. The grey, then featureless flank of the building on the extreme right is the rear of Nos 33–34 Oxford Street, the former Oxford public house, listed as such in the last 1975 *Kelly's Directory*, and as the Oxford Spirit Stores from 1875 to 1954. In keeping with much of Oxford Street now, it is another restaurant, named (rather confusingly, given its immediate neighbour) as the 'Oxford Brasserie'. From the location where I took the first photograph, the north façade of the white-fronted 1927 South Western House extension still looms over the rooftops in the background, and one can just glimpse the letters 'CU' of Cunard, who still used it as their head office. The radio antennae on the roof denote that it was also the local BBC headquarters. As can be seen, the entire space between Terminus Terrace (just out of the picture on the left), and John Street itself in the foreground, is derelict and awaiting redevelopment. Also, take note of the row of parking meters. In the second picture, taken in 2014, three-storey terrace 'townhouses' have since been built here (and also along the south side of Bernard Street). Although they do at least make *some* architectural concession to the older nineteenth-century terraces, they are still rather bland. They also completely block out any attempt to exactly replicate the previous view.

Platform, Town Quay & Trafalgar Dock

Next page: The inset, opposite (taken *c.* 1986, viewed here from Lower Canal Walk), is of No. 1 Orchard Place, also known as Bowling Green House. From May 1974 onward occupied by Wainwright Bros. & Co. Ltd, a family firm of international shipping and port agents founded in 1889, whose current CEO, since 2006, is Tim Wainwright. Previously they had been based at No. 20 Queens Terrace, where, in 1951, a Mr Edward Alderson had been appointed the German Honorary Consul; the connection with Wainwright Bros being that they acted as port agents to a large number of German shipowners. The German Consulate also moved to Orchard Place, where it remained until 2012 when Mr Alderson's successor, Mr Roger Thornton, retired, having been Honorary Consul for thirty-six years since 1976. It was only with his successor, Mr Richard Cutler, that the German Consulate moved to its current address in Totton. Not only were visitors on consular business seen in the Wainwright Bros meeting room, but the receptionist also doubled her duties to help the Consul. At the time of his appointment, Mr Thornton (aged thirty-two) was the youngest German *Honorarkonsul* and, upon retirement, the longest serving of the 450 German Honorary Consuls worldwide. Bowling Green House, now a Grade II listed building built in the mid-nineteenth century, was brick with a green slate roof and a distinctive weathervane.

In 2014, the German Consulate may have gone, but Wainwright Bros are still there, seen here (my thanks to the current 'Master of the Green') in an unusual angle from inside the walled Old Bowling Green. It is reputed to be the oldest in the world, in use since 1299, when it was established by King Richard I for the 'recreational use' of the Warden of God's House Hospital. Since 1776, there is a unique annual 'Knighthood' competition held, the winner being entitled 'Knight of the Green' and addressed as 'sir', although thereafter banned from future competition. In 1985, Lower Canal Walk (on the left; Orchard Place and Queens Park are on the right) was another area that was rather shabby and run down, but from 1994 until 2008 saw massive residential redevelopment along Canal Walk itself, along with Briton Street between Telephone House and the junction with Queens Terrace. The nearest building is Carpathia Court (No. 6 Briton Street), while beyond that is City Court, and, on the right, the thirteen-storey, 280-apartment Oceania Boulevard, a much more attractive occupant of this corner site then the 1960s Customs House, which had formerly been the regional headquarters for HM Customs & Excise.

Looking across to Town Quay from the then semi-derelict shed and wharf between Trafalgar Dock and Town Quay pier in November 1985, not long before everything seen here in the foreground was swept away for redevelopment. The medieval God's House and Tower are on the extreme right, half out of the picture, with the nineteenth-century Tower House and Solent House next door. In 2011, it was being used as a 'workspace for creative arts', seen again from the Back of the Walls. Beyond that, is the solid-looking two-storey Clyde Buildings, which was occupied by maritime companies but then converted into flats. Continuing the parade, out of this picture, is what was once a one-storey snack bar and diner, and is incorporated into the Platform Tavern, the main building having three storeys. This was originally opened in 1872, but suffered bomb damage in November 1940. It reopened in 1954 and was refurbished in 1988. Since 1997 it had been a pub, restaurant and music venue, with its own in-house brewery, trading as the Dancing Man Brewery. In 2014, the current owners won the concession to convert the medieval Wool House (the former Maritime Museum) into a similar pub restaurant. Continuing this parade, Eastgate House was once the furnishing workshops for Edwin Jones & Co. (now Debenhams), until badly damaged in 1940. At one time in the post-war period, it was a printing works, and even now it is still mostly given over to office space. Finally, still there in the 1980s, with a bomb site on either side, was The Sun public house, formerly The Sun Hotel, destroyed in 1940 and rebuilt in 1944 as a flat-roofed, single-storey 'temporary' structure, on the original eighteenth-century foundations. It continued until June 1990, when it finally closed. It was boarded up and derelict for another four years, until 1994, when it was eventually demolished. The late-1990s office block, Notobene House (named after the medieval tower which once stood on this site), now occupies this entire site between Town Quay and Winkle Street.

This and next page: The first picture was taken in 1985 (the same white building can be seen in the previous picture), however, everything on the left – with the exception of the Harbour House, the Harbour Board Office in the distance – was demolished soon after. Admittedly, the buildings were, for the most part, a jumble of essentially purely functional, post-war, nondescript commercial structures of little architectural merit, and perhaps visually did little to enhance the historic nature of the fourteenth- and fifteenth-century God's House town gateway and tower, a Grade II listed building, which, from 1961 until 2011, housed Southampton's Museum of Archaeology. The three (seemingly nameless) four-storey, postmodern, two-tone brick office buildings that replaced them around 1988 are certainly attractive, but perhaps yet again this is an opportunity lost. Harbour House was built in 1924/25, on the site of a previous nineteenth-century harbour office (the basements of the earlier building apparently being incorporated into the new one), and was designed in the Edwardian baroque style by the then borough engineer, E. Cooper Poole. The cupola on the central tower is topped by a globe weathervane, apparently with the appropriate inscription in Latin, *Janua Maris* – 'Gateway to the Sea'. A later, post-war extension at the rear was also demolished in the late-1980s. Sadly, in 2001, this landmark building (to use the city council town planners' favourite phrase) was sold to developers and, until 2012, it was Maxim's restaurant and casino, with a nightclub called Club Rosso in the new rear extension (built 2003). In 2014, it is the Playhouse Gentlemen's Club, basically a glorified strip club. Having already lost out on using the former cross-Channel ferry terminal in Ocean Village (which was subsequently demolished and the Harbour Lights Cinema now occupying this site), with imagination and a tasteful (perhaps glass) rear annex extension, this would have made the perfect maritime museum to replace the, by then, already inadequate Wool House. SeaCity, in the Civic Centre, is the wrong place – both historically and architecturally. The planted trees and attractive street furniture in the later (*c.* 2008) picture shows a marked contrast to the mundane indifference to such things seen just a few years earlier. In 2014, long overdue road improvements are being undertaken between West Quay Road and the Queens Terrace/Canute Road junction, only now fulfilling proposals made as long ago as 1985.

The Town Quay office development in 1988, the three buildings still not yet occupied. The exterior design is attractive, visually interesting and vaguely nautical. Cranes and old docks buildings could still be seen off to the right. The same view today is comparatively unchanged; the buildings appear to have only numbers, rather than names, but the view behind is now dominated by metal fences and car parks, with the new silver Cunard Ocean Terminal building, opened in May 2009, beyond. However, and especially with all retail outlets and most catering having vanished from the late-1980s Town Quay redevelopment itself, and the failure to properly develop the area around Trafalgar Dock or build any (never mind affordable) housing, again as promised, this area is still rather sterile, devoid of any real life or activity.

Here follow just some of a number of photographs I took in November 1985 of the old Town Quay 'Dock Gate 6', and the brick warehouses on the pier – all of which were very shortly to be swept away for the new Town Quay development. Late nineteenth-century photographs show the Quay pier almost empty of buildings; these buildings date from the 1920s or early 1930s. In the foreground can still be seen the railway lines that originally ran across Canute Road, south of Platform Road, and on towards West Quay Road. They have vanished along with everything else seen here, although it was still possible until a few years ago to see one surviving fragment between the Western Esplanade/West Quay Road roundabout and Mayflower Park. The sign on the wall reads, 'Mayflower Oilfield Services Ltd', and below it a smaller sign specifies a 15 mph speed limit.

Continuing the time sequence; the same view, first in *c.* 1987/88, of the main entrance to the new Town Quay development in its all-too-brief heyday. 'MARINA – SHOPS – BARS – RESTAURANTS – FERRIES', proclaims the sign. It was possible to walk right through, along a delightful, covered pedestrian shopping street, past the Hythe and Red Jet ferry terminal, with more shop units on the right, out into a open piazza with views across the top end of the new marina to the arms of the Trafalgar Dock Quay opposite, while the Around the World pub closed the view out across the Test. Another failure of imagination: while the old brick warehouses, seen in the previous picture and again viewed along the pier, were perhaps 'not fit for purpose', but surely the attractive stone and brick front building could easily have been incorporated into the new structure instead of the rather bland reception wing seen here on the right. Yet again an opportunity lost (like the possibility of preserving one of dock cranes) to retain at least something of the old architecture.

Fast forward another few years, the last photograph is dated 2007, but apart from the recent appearance of a Starbucks coffee house facing the roadway on the right, and the disappearance of the sheltered pedestrian walkway beyond that, little else has changed. Following its phase two incarnation, the main entrance is now no longer open for the general public, leading instead to commercial offices, divided into four distinct units, each with their own separate entrances, known as Beresford House, Waterside House, Medina Chambers and Ariadne House. The wall plaque, erected in 1994, commemorates the connection of Town Quay with the D-Day landings fifty years earlier.

Two pictures, forming a panorama of the various sheds and warehouses on Town Quay pier, as viewed *c.* 1985/86, from the direction of the Red Funnel Isle of Wight terminal. It is almost impossible now to imagine Town Quay bustling with the loading and unloading of coastal and cross-channel cargo ships, and with railway tracks (originally on both sides of the cargo sheds) running the full length of the pier. By the 1960s, it is said that partly due to new motorway links, this coastal traffic had dramatically declined. However, an example of how Town Quay was, in its time, at the cutting-edge of innovation was the introduction of electric cranes in 1893, apparently the first of their kind on any British quayside, and only decommissioned in 1950. Once again, thirty or forty years on, a complete failure of any forethought or imagination has meant so much of the city's potential maritime heritage has been lost.

Behind the front office façade, next to Dock Gate 6 (seen on the extreme left in the first picture), the sheds stretched back virtually the full length of the pier, and were rather shabby by the 1980s, essentially functional. The sheds seen here were being used by Williams Shipping, established in 1894, and still based at Millbrook – the name appears on the blue hatchway doors next to the painted 'J' on the brickwork, and on the moored boat next to the crane. In the second picture, one of the Red Funnel 'Shearwater' hydrofoils can be seen moored in the right foreground. The two tug-like craft moored to the pier are both registered in Cowes and, according to Colin Williams, the current joint managing director of Williams Shipping Holdings Ltd, they are the *Wilbernia* and *Murius*, 'barges used to deliver ships stores to tankers on Fawley jetty'.

Next page: Two more comparisons, the first being another 1985 photograph of the Town Quay pier, this time from the opposite side to that previous, viewed from next to the Harbour Board building, and the same view as seen in 2007. Town Quay (together with the Royal Pier and Mayflower Park) might be described as something of a 'tale of two cities' between Southampton and Portsmouth, illustrating the glaring contrast in how they have promoted their respective waterfronts. Opened in 2001, fifteen years on from Town Quay's inception, and (for all its own limitations and general commercialism) Portsmouth's Gunwharf Quays still shows how it *might* have been. It has successfully combined housing, leisure and commercial facilities, lively retail outlets, enticing restaurants right across the price-range, together with the preservation of many of the more attractive pre-existing buildings – and even a crane! Something Town Quay *could* have done, but sadly, did not. All this, plus plenty of traffic-free pedestrian access to the waterfront. So, back in Southampton, what went wrong? It might be too simplistic to say that the sole villain of the piece is ABP. One has to ask if there was not also, at the heart of the original design, both a lack of a real political will, together with a fundamental failure of imagination. To refer again to the 1985 City Planning Department proposals for Town Quay:

> This area is mainly vacant or under-used dockland, but includes the terminus for the Hythe ferry and adjoins the jetties, marshalling areas and car parks occupied by Red Funnel. It has special assets which can be exploited to make a major impact in rejuvenating the Lower Town. The enclosed water frontage [between Town Quay and Trafalgar Quay] is well located for development as a marina. The extensive water frontages offer new opportunities for public access and the potential for an exciting and commercially viable development ... Major uses will include offices and housing and could include a hotel. Some shops, restaurants, pubs and clubs should be included in development on the quay itself. This will be a splendid viewpoint of activity on the river, the marina and the Old Town, replacing the decaying Royal Pier. Therefore, an essential component of development proposals must be a public promenade which is attractive to use. This should extend along the whole length of the Quay terminating at a public viewpoint with panoramas over the Test.

It then goes on to say that the future of the Hythe ferry be safeguarded, which is perhaps one of the few stipulations in the above proposals that were actually adhered to. The shops and pubs came and went. The Around the World pub at the very end of the development was irrationally designed and built so as not to give any opportunity of viewing that 'panorama over the Test'. It eventually closed in 2006. The pedestrian promenade, such as it is, still involves running the gauntlet of motor cars, while the views of the marina are effectively off limits, except from the distance. The hotel never materialised, and neither did any affordable public housing. However, the 'decaying Royal Pier' is still there, more awful than ever. Of the restaurants, only two have survived – the Italian restaurant La Margherita moved here from Commercial Road (*see below*), taking the most prominent spot when the phase 2 refurbishment blocked off the former main entrance. Clocking up twenty years of residency, Monsieur Hulot, a family-run coffee shop opposite the Hythe and Isle of Wight ferry terminals, has survived against the odds, despite having its previous thoroughfare rather brutally severed. In 2013, a Starbucks coffee house has opened on the right-hand side corner, and hot snacks, newspapers and confectionery can be purchased from the opposite the ferry. At least Ocean Village has still a glimmer of life; Town Quay, especially compared to its brief late 1980s heyday, is dreary and dead. Even the 'public viewpoint' at the very end of the pier has been fenced off for much of the last ten years. In 2011, a proposed £3 million revamp was a total waste of money and effort, aiming only to improve the marina, rather than attracting locals back. Quite the opposite. The year 2012 saw the introduction of 'Big Brother'-style CCTV cameras, which now record and log the coming and going of every motor vehicle on the Quay; failure to purchase a parking ticket results in an automatically generated minimum £70 fine – 'new opportunities for public access', it isn't.

This and next page: Three pictures, all taken *c.* 1985/86, form a panorama view of Berth 51 and the old Harland and Wolff ship repair sheds, behind which is Trafalgar Dock, as viewed from Town Quay. The 912-ft (278 m) long Trafalgar Dry Dock (later designated Dock No. 6) was opened on 21 October 1905 (hence its name, commemorating the 100th anniversary of the battle), while the Belfast-based Harland and Wolff first opened their repair facilities here in 1907, but by 1963 they were already being run down, only to close completely in 1973. However, it is still possible to read the now faded 'Harland & Wolff Limited' name on the roof, most noticeably in the second picture. Nothing now remains of this huge complex, which extended back to Atlantic Way (where Dock Gate 4 is now). The last time Trafalgar Dock was used for ship repairs was in 1989 and, although Grade II listed in 1988, apparently the philistines at ABP filled in 90 per cent, turning it into a surface car park, leaving only the dock gate. Having been enlarged in 1913 and again in 1922, it was at one time the largest dry dock in the world. Between 2010 and 2012, ambitious plans were underway to locate the AeroNautica Museum here, replacing the now rather neglected Solent Sky (the former Aviation Museum) from its current site in Albert Road South, but (typically) these appear to have fallen through. Alternative proposals suggest the Red Funnel Ferry terminal moving here, but, again, as with thirty-year-old promises to improve Mayflower Park, we've been here before.

Everything in the first two pictures has been swept away and even the shoreline has altered; the foreground is now Town Quay Marina, with its concrete breakwater and pontoons. While the semi-derelict shabbiness of the workaday sheds and wharfs may have gone, the foreshore on the left now comprises rocks, seaweed and stagnant slimy water. The former Harland and Wolff site is now nothing more than just a series of gigantic car parks closed off from each other by ugly metal fencing. What was Trafalgar Dock is now dominated by the latest generation of the various Cunard liners, and the rather unimpressive 2009 Ocean Terminal – basically just a long, silver shed. The previous and much admired Art Deco Ocean Terminal, designed by C. B. Dromgoole, a humble architect from the then chief docks engineer's department, opened in 1950, was wantonly demolished in 1983.

The last picture continues the panorama, actually taken from the Town Quay pier, looking beyond berth 50 towards the silos next to berth 47, which date from 1982. The white building glimpsed behind the foreground metal gantry was the old BOAC seaplane terminal building. Even now, the four piers of the Floating Dock are still visible, which were later used by seaplanes until the early 1950s.

The Red Funnel ferry terminal, as seen in November 1985. In the foreground, moored either side of the pontoon, are two of the *Shearwater* hydrofoils, first introduced in 1969, the original *Shearwater* and *Shearwater I* being Italian-built and capable of carrying fifty-four passengers. Seen here on the right is *Shearwater 4*, introduced in 1973, known as the RH70, with a capacity for sixty-seven passengers. *Shearwater 5* and *6* entered service in 1982, but with the introduction of the larger, 138-passenger Red Jet catamarans in 1991, the hydrofoils were all withdrawn by 1998. In the background on the left is one of the then car ferry fleets. At this time there were three: *MV Cowes Castle* (1965–94), *MV Norris Castle III* (1968–94) and *MV Netley Castle* (1974–97). On the right of the picture is the foot passenger gantry – not too different today. Dating back to 1820, since 1861 the company name has been The Southampton, Isle of Wight and South of England Royal Mail Steam Packet Co. Ltd, but it has been better known as Red Funnel (after its distinctive livery) since 1935. In 1989, it was subject to a hostile takeover bid by rival ferry company Sally Lines, thwarted by becoming part of Allied British Ports Holdings. In 2001, typifying the corporate world we live in, where once established companies are little more than Monopoly pieces, it was sold to J. P. Morgan Partners Inc., then in 2004 to the Bank of Scotland (for £60 million), only to be sold again by HBOS to Prudential's Infracapital division in 2007, this time for £200 million.

Back of the Walls, High Street & the Bargate Centre

This and previous page: God's House Tower on the left, the rear of Tower House (centre) and Solent House (on the right), with Winkle Street extending right, as viewed from Back of the Walls, *c.* 1986. Despite the presence of the Museum of Archaeology (opened in 1950, closed 2011), this area, to quote the 1985 City Planning Department leaflet of 'policies and proposals', 'run-down and ... uninviting ... particularly along Back-of-the-Walls, Gloucester Passage and Lower Canal Walk'. Indeed, even the lower half of the High Street, certainly from the new post-war Castle Way/Briton Street to Town Quay, continued to look shabby, derelict and unfulfilled right up until the late 1990s, fifty years after what was described as 'the most beautiful High Street in England' was extensively destroyed by bombs. Both Tower House and Solent House date from the early nineteenth century. A wall plaque on Solent House reads '1822 – G. A. M.', apparently the initials of the town mayor (*in the picture above, taken in 2011*), when the buildings were known as Solent Cottage and Platform House. Tower House may have traces of a building from the previous century, before this part of the town walls was pulled down in *c.* 1803/04. Like God's House, they were at one time part of the Bridewell, or town prison, which closed in 1854/55. It is believed that Tower House was probably reconstructed between 1846 and 1870. Work was already underway to improve this locality, and the eventual result can be seen in the second picture (*above*), taken in 2011.

This and next page: More views from *c.* 1986, this time actually of Back of the Walls, looking across to Gloucester Square, with the grey, L-shaped Telephone House. Built around 1967, this was the British Telecom headquarters, dominating the east side of the High Street, although its main entrance was onto Briton Street, which, up until the Second World War, had been just a narrow alleyway linking Canal Walk with Queen's Terrace, roughly where City Court and Oceana Boulevard are now. Gloucester Square, now a surface car park with 90 spaces, also used to be much smaller. The whole of this area was a tight cluster of working-class residential dwellings, small shops and pubs, which, even in the 1930s, was threatened with demolition. In medieval times, this had been the site of a Franciscan friary, founded in 1237, whose water system, which was fed by pipes from springs to the north, was shared with the town's inhabitants. However, by the time of the dissolution in 1538, there were only six inmates, and the sale raised only 32s. In 1740, a sugar refinery was built here, and the 1910 Ordance Survey shows a now lost narrow alleyway called Sugarhouse Lane, which emerged into the High Street opposite Broad Lane. Most of the warehouses were destroyed in 1940, but a few survived into the 1990s, as seen here along the south flank of Gloucester Square facing the High Street. Only in the last dozen years has all the area between the square itself and the rear of St Julian's Chapel in Winkle Street been tastefully redeveloped for housing and apartments, gradually bringing life back into this part of the Old Town. A good example of architectural compatibility between the ancient and modern can be seen in the curved, stone-fronted façade of what is probably the stairwell of the newer building, which mirrors that of the ruined fourteenth-century Round Tower immediately opposite.

In the 1980s, British Telecom expanded into Friary House, the red-brick annex seen here on the right, but, by the late 1990s, such was the rapid pace of change in telephone and communications technology, they were eventually able to contract their entire operations into the smaller building (which they still occupy). The larger building was completely re-clad and remodelled by Linden Homes (with a very attractive and innovative design), into 128 one-, two- and three-bedroom apartments, still named Telephone House, with a ground-floor pharmacy. The height of the medieval wall in the top picture opposite (with what looks like a Second World War blockhouse) suggests that this photograph was taken from Lower Canal Walk, the area between the two having also since been developed in the 1990s by attractive and visually varied five- and six-storey housing.

This and next page: Here are two views of the High Street, both seen from the junction of Briton Street, contrasting the significant, long-overdue change to this part of Southampton since the late 1980s and now. The first photograph, taken in January 1986, with the spire of St Michael's church visible above the roofline, shows the simple, but still attractive, brick-built Marconi Marine building at No. 107 High Street (built *c.* 1966). The curved side extends back along Castle Way, where, on the extreme left, No. 58 French Street can be seen. This was once the Bull's Head public house, since 1988 a museum – the 'Medieval Merchant's House' – one of the oldest buildings in the city. It was built in 1290 by John Fortin, and is one of the earliest surviving merchant houses in England. Badly damaged in 1940 (by which time, one source says, it was being used as a brothel), it was subsequently boarded-up and semi-derelict until eventually taken over and restored to former glory by English Heritage in 1984. Out of sight on the left, at No. 65 Castle Way, was the Mayflower, a Whitbread public house, while on the right, down from the Marconi building (and the now almost extinct cherry-red K8 telephone boxes first introduced 1968) was Nos 108–112, A. G. Benfield Wholesale Greengrocers, with Habitat (Nos 113–118) beyond that.

Built between 1961 and 1963, the inner ring road saw Portland Terrace extended south beyond Bargate Street, continuing on as Castle Way, slicing through the old pre-war streets and alleyways of Landsdown Hill and swallowing up part of French Street. It then curved into the High Street, where a new, wider and longer version of Briton Street then took traffic eastwards, towards Queen's Terrace. However, part of the long overdue redevelopment of the lower High Street from 2002 onwards saw Castle Way blend back into French Street. Traffic was now fed into the High Street further north from West Street, with a new pedestrian walkway leading directly from the High Street, opposite the old Post Office building directly through to the Medieval Merchant's House. The previous view from the junction of Briton Street is now transformed. While, as with Portsmouth, one might lament the loss of the pre-war architectural elegance and variety of the High Street as it was, at least these buildings in particular (opposite Goldsmith Court) have a postmodern elegance. It is now Castle Place, with a ground-floor Co-operative food store and commercial offices at street level, apartments with balconies (again by Linden Homes) and a busy, but interesting, façade above.

Bargate and Bargate Street viewed from the High Street, October 1985. The wonderful twentieth-century Bargate is beloved by Southampton citizens and visitors alike; it even features in the city's emblem. However, to generations of town planners and modernists, the Bargate, along with other medieval and pre-Victorian relics, has more often been a nuisance, an anachronism in the way of 'progress'. It might seem incredible now that even in the early decades of the twentieth century, there were some who wanted to demolish it or sell it to the Americans. The buildings on the east side were cleared away in the early 1930s and, by the 1950s, right through to the early 1990s, when the east side was pedestrianised again, historic Bargate was little more than a glorified traffic island. Only very recently was the west side eventually closed off to traffic, while the long-term plan (first mooted in 2009) is for both the pre-war East Bargate/Hanover Buildings and post-war buildings of West Bargate (seen here) to be completely redeveloped into a traffic-free piazza with the Bargate again linked by a pedestrian walkway to the surviving medieval walls. Watch this space.

In 1984, No. 184 High Street was a Huckleberry's Burger Bar (first introduced from America into the UK in 1980), but that year the bars were sold and converted into Wimpy bars (operating under licence to J. Lyons in the UK since 1954). In 1977, they were owned by United Biscuits, but, by the late 1980s, Wimpy was losing ground to McDonald's, who opened their first restaurant in 1974. In Southampton, Wimpy and McDonald's faced each other, the latter (until they moved to WestQuay) being on the corner of Hanover Buildings, next to the Halifax Building Society. Finally, in 1989, the Wimpy chain was sold to Grand Metropolitan (now Diageo), who had acquired Burger King the year before. It was they who converted all their Wimpy counter service restaurants into Burger King, as they remain today.

Even more so than the rise and fall of Ocean Village and Town Quay, the Bargate Centre probably symbolised the hopes and possibilities in the new emerging Southampton. It was briefly the trailblazer for a multitude of ideas to drag Southampton into the late-twentieth century. Most of these, like the Metro 2000 project, or glassing-over Guildhall Square and Above Bar Street beyond the junction of Civic Centre Road and New Road, never got beyond the drawing board. Bargate Centre proved successful at first, especially the atrium area, which formed a link between York Gate and East Street. Its lower-floor internet café, vaguely Egyptian/Art Deco statues and the various shops all catered for the more eclectic tastes in alternative fashion. But gradually (like Town Quay) all were to succumb to increased overheads and perhaps a limited clientele, so that one by one they were extinguished.

More foolish business ventures included a newsagent on the top atrium level, where no one went – it vanished again within months. Increasingly it became a mere cut-through, sad and increasingly lifeless and, one by one, units fell empty. The terminal decline had set in. Sega Park attracted the young, and in 1997 a controversial, outright ageist advertising campaign actively discouraged 'old' people – not the best way to encourage footfalls, one would have thought. The cheap home computer, laptop and iPhone saw the demand for an cyber café gradually vanish, while the lower-floor atrium café also went from being a pleasant eatery, to (briefly) a smokers' refuge, and finally (and this time all too briefly), a Filipino diner. The two photographs reproduced here are of the atrium area, taken by the author in 1989, very soon after it opened. Unfortunately, most of the rest of the set have been lost.

This and next page: Back in 1984, the proposal to develop the old Cooper's Brewery site started with such promise, bravely focusing on 'specialist outlets rather than mainstream'. Its attractive and spacious, slightly curving, two-level mall led to a three-level atrium, beyond which was access to the multi-storey car park; the architecture did at least incorporate the surviving town walls in York Walk, and what little (sadly) remained of York Gate; it also (shades of the Marlands Centre and the recreated fragment of Manchester Terrace) reproduced the historic Nos. 1 and 2 York Buildings (reputed to have once been lived in by T. E. Lawrence). But even by the time it opened in 1989, a harsher economic retail reality was setting in, and the ambitious next phase to extend covered shopping into Queensway never materialised. In total it comprised 40 retail units, over 70,000 square feet (6,503 square metres), with 300 car parking spaces. The interior design (by Fitch & Co., with architects W. H. Saunders & Son) was light, modern, airy and pure Art Deco.

Having already been sold to the European property giant Parkridge Holdings in 2008 for £17.25 million, in 2009 another ambitious plan was put forward to demolish both the late 1950s Debenhams department store, known as Queen's Building, located in Queensway (which would then have been redeveloped with a residential tower block). The plan was to build a brand new Debenhams store on the Bargate Centre site, which would be constructed as part of a new 'covered street' (a new spin on the original 1984 plan) linking Bargate with Queensway. However, this proposal was scrapped when, in 2011, Debenhams opted to revamp their existing store instead. By then there were only eleven retailers still trading, and Parkridge (Bargate) Ltd went into liquidation. In February 2013 the receivers, BNP Paribas Real Estate, having failed to secure a buyer, finally closed the centre completely. The 2014 photographs show the three entrances, in East Bargate, York Gate and Strand Street, now boarded up. Currently, the building's fate is still unknown, subject only to rumour. Nos 2–6 High Street, immediately to the right of the East Bargate entrance, was still, until 2014, owned by the Montague Burton Group (gentlemen's outfitters), but had been latterly occupied by Jongleurs, a cocktail bar/nightclub on the ground floor, with a comedy club above. Built in 1937, by Braziers & Sons for £11,000, in the Art Nouveau style, this building was a Red Cross centre for US troops during the Second World War.

Westgate, Portland Terrace & West Quay Centre

This and previous page: Two pictures of Westgate Street, viewed from the direction of Cuckoo Lane, taken forty years apart. The first photograph (from when I visited Southampton to see friends who lived here) was certainly taken before 1975, as the 1973–75 restoration to the old building (seen on the left) removed the upper-storey battens to reveal the timber-frame beams underneath. The second picture (deliberately a wider view) is as it is now, in 2014. Apart from the two 'period' cars, and perhaps the concrete bollards, the 1970s view might still seem almost Victorian – uneven cobbled roadway, the architecture rude and rather shabby, overgrown shrub on the right. Only the ugly, Brutalist, thirteen-storey, grey concrete Castle House (built 1962) disrupts the view – another breathtaking example of either mindless civic stupidity, or a typically calculated Modernist attempt to not just ignore the past, but try and obliterate it. The so-called Tudor Merchant's Hall on the left was originally situated in St Michael's Square, with a fish market on the ground floor, and, being from pre-1410, actually predates the Tudor period by at least thirty-five years. In 1634, it was derelict and sold to Edward Exton for 'twenty marks' (just over £13) taken down and re-erected here. It has been used as a warehouse, store and even a temporary mortuary during and after D-Day, but is now renamed Westgate Hall and is hired out as a venue for concerts, conferences and wedding receptions. Even less than a century ago, the old fourteenth-century West Gate still opened directly out onto the water, but now Western Esplanade is little more than a car park, while the traffic roars along West Quay Road, and the view is blocked off by the Grand Harbour Hotel and The Quays (Eddie Read) swimming and leisure complex.

No. 8 Portland House, the southern end of the parade, which includes Nos 8–16, viewed from Portland Street opposite (*c.* 1987-88), with the North Arundel Towers looming behind. Apparently neither the architect, nor the city council town planner, responsible for the 1967–69 Arundel Towers blocks (*see below*), had thought about the sheer discrepancy of style and scale that should have been blatantly obvious. Not, of course, did the Modernist architect, who designs with little thought or concern to his creation's impact on the surroundings. Even detractors of the gigantic WestQuay shopping centre, which has since replaced Arundel Towers, would probably concede the postmodern building is a bit more in keeping with its surroundings, and Nos 8–10 are now actually the WestQuay management suite, while Nos 12–16 are flats. Originally Portland Terrace had ended in a cul-de-sac, roughly where the WestQuay shops now cross over the road, with the former Royal Victoria Assembly Rooms (dating from 1820), blocking off the end. Everything opposite and to the south, including the assembly rooms, was demolished in 1961 when the inner ring road was constructed. Nos 8–16 Portland Terrace were built around 1835, and they comprise four storeys and a basement, with the rear elevation being five storeys, and hung with Devonshire slate. Nos 1–13, and Nos 23–25 Portland Street date from 1830, and all were listed for Grade II protection in 1953, thereby preserving this tiny bit of late-Regency period Southampton for posterity.

Just a sample of the series of photographs, all taken from the footbridge (itself constructed in 1990) connecting the medieval town walls over Portland Terrace, recording the 1997–99 process of demolition, prior to the subsequent construction of, the WestQuay shopping centre which was eventually opened in autumn 2000. For a modern pub, the drum-like Dog and Duck public house (built 1968, originally called the Arundel Centre Inn) was not without some architectural merit, and I remember going there occasionally to eat. Originally a Bass Charrington pub, it later became a free house, and apparently its night-time guise included a nightclub called Barbarella's, aka Thursday's. Located in the sunken area where the circular Waterstone's/Costa Coffee patio is now, it could perhaps have been successfully incorporated into the new development.

This and next page: These images show a 1967–69 South and North Arundel Towers, a huge fourteen-storey grey concrete and glass project, each 50,000 square feet (4,645 square metres). They were both constructed between Portland Terrace (where the main structure was poised on the kind of massive concrete *pilotis* so beloved by the modernist guru Le Corbusier), and the lower Western Esplanade, with its depressingly brutal, almost Berlin Wall-like multi-storey 800-capacity car park. The South Tower housed the local headquarters for Barclay's Bank, plus the offices for Esso Chemicals and Southern Ferries and Normandy Ferries, while the North Tower housed various local government offices (both Hampshire County Council and Southampton City Council), as well the Royal Insurance Group and the publishers of Yellow Pages. The architects were R. Seifert & Partners. Richard Seifert (1910–2001), is perhaps best known for Centre Point in London, having earned the description of 'having had more influence on the London skyline than anyone since Wren', with his numerous uncompromising modernist tower blocks. While he is still highly regarded by lovers of this style, many of his 'masterpieces', such as Drapers Gardens near Throgmorton Street, or the National Westminster Tower, have since been either demolished or drastically remodelled out of all recognition.

As seen here around 2003, taken from the same location as the previous two pictures, WestQuay shopping centre finally opened in September 2000. On the left is Waterstones, having moved here from the former Dillons Bookshop (rebranded in 1999) in Hanover Buildings. It now occupies two floors, the lower patio level (which it shares with Costa Coffee) and the Portland Terrace atrium entrance level. On the right is the concrete frontage of four-storey City Wall House, built 1968/69. *Kelly's* for 1971 to 1975 has the occupant as the Southern Gas Board. The GO-AD maps for 1983–88 lists the occupant as Prime Computer, a Massachusetts-based minicomputer manufacturer trading from 1972–92. Thereafter, from 1993 right through the 1990s, it was vacant, and it still is, but now even the building name has gone. Beyond that is the entrance to Spa Road, now only leading to the rear pedestrian entrance of Boots, and a delivery area for the Above Bar Street shops. Both the Spa Tavern (No. 16 Spa Road, dating from the 1850s, once a Cooper's Brewery pub), and the Wig and Pen (Whitbread) have vanished, as has the passageway through to the old *Daily Echo* building.

Looking north along the new Harbour Parade, *c.* 1999/early 2000, at what would be the Marks & Spencer's wing of WestQuay on the right, and the main pedestrian entrance and footbridge across to the multi-storey car park (*out of the picture, left*). Looking beyond the raised roof of the main central atrium, the soon-to-be John Lewis wing is in the far distance, facing Pirelli Street. They continue to constitute the two major 'anchor' stores. At street level, already visible behind the construction fences, can be see the attractive flint stone rendering, behind which is now the three-tier internal WestQuay car park – what a visual contrast to the stark concrete brutalism of the old Arundel Towers multi-storey car park that was once here! The sign on the bridge read Sir Robert McAlpine, although the developer was Chapmen, Taylor & Partners. The property owner is Hammerson plc, whose portfolio also includes the Birmingham Bullring and Brent Cross.

Just one of around eighty photographs I took within days of WestQuay opening at the end of September 2000, this of the central atrium and top-floor food terrace. Now, following the 2012 refurbishment, it has been rebranded with the more up-market title, 'Dining Level'. There are two shopping floors and three more car parking levels below this. Within a few weeks of me taking these photographs (where no one challenged me), uniformed security officers would try and enforce a 'no photography' bye-law. However, in recent years (perhaps belatedly acknowledging that all the world and his dog now have cameras in their mobile phones and laptops) I no longer see this vigilance. Given the enormous crowds, especially at weekends, the three glass central elevators connecting the lower toilets and car park levels are often not enough, while the escalators are so placed to necessitate a semi-circular walk past lots of tempting shops, just to get up or down to the next level. McDonald's is still there (although having been consolidated back to one floor), while the palm trees have gone and once public open balcony terrace beyond the glass window is now reserved exclusively for diners of Café Rouge and Café Giardino. Harry Ramsden's fish and chips moved here from Ocean Village to occupy a permanent position on the upper mezzanine level, behind the lifts on the left. Costa Coffee has three outlets here, their busiest being again on the left, next to the lifts. At 800,000 square feet (70,000 square metres), six floors high and with 150 stores, and extending 400 metres from Above Bar Street to Harbour Parade, WestQuay is one of the largest shopping centres in the South of England, outside of London. Probably more than anything else since the construction of the Western Docks and the destruction in the Second World War, WestQuay has totally transformed Southampton having not just realigned its commercial and retail heart westward rather than north–south (and having a decade-long impact with empty retail units in and around Above Bar Street), but also having affected the city's overall topography and physical appearance.

This view is looking along Western Esplanade from the vantage point of the medieval Arundel Tower, *c.* 1998/99. Now it is already quite difficult to recollect the Esplanade before WestQuay blocked it off, continuing on uninterrupted past the once extensive Pirelli-General cables works to the junction with Civil Centre Road. In the middle distance can be seen the 173-room, 4-star Grand Harbour Hotel (until 2013 part of the De Vere Group), which opened in 1994, with the tip of its iconic glass pyramid atrium facing towards the waterfront just visible over the roofline. On the right, just across West Quay Road, is what is now the 125-room Holiday Inn (since 2003 part of the InterContinental Hotels Group), which was formerly the Post House, at one time part of the Trust House Forte Group. Built in 1965 and opened in 1966, it was originally the Skyways Hotel. The architectural contrast between the two hotels is striking.

The construction site and crane seen here was for the new swimming baths complex, now known as The Quays swimming and diving complex, opened in 2000 to replace the previous glass-fronted Olympic-size Central Baths, which had opened in 1961, and had been designed by then borough architect, L. Berger. He had also built Millbank Tower, the first of Southampton's post-war tower blocks. In the 1980s, Central Baths was rebranded as 'Centre 2000', and a flume was added with the novelty of actually being outside the original building. Sadly, heating costs became prohibitive and it finally closed in 1992. The building was boarded up and fell into disrepair, even at one time being used by squatters and gypsies, until it was finally ignominiously demolished in 1997. Unfortunately, the £10 million replacement has all the glamour and openness of a rather dismal factory or warehouse. Unlike its predecessor, the interior is without any natural light, and it feels extremely claustrophobic – where was the architectural imagination of its neighbour, the Grand Harbour Hotel?

Above Bar Street & the
Marlands Centre

This and previous page: The attractive Portland stone façade of the purpose-built post-war *Southern Evening Echo* offices and printworks, at what was Nos 41–45 Above Bar Street. This photograph was taken in January 1986, with the Spa Road passageway seen on the left. Tony Gallaher's *Southampton Since 1945* (part of the *Britain in Old Photographs* series, published originally by Sutton Publishing, 1998) has a fascinating 1953 photograph of this building under construction, with just the girder framework. The previous *Southern Echo* building was destroyed in November 1940, after which production moved to its sister newspaper in Bournemouth. This new building was constructed in 1952–55, with the production plant and editorial offices facing onto Portland Street opening first. It was eventually officially opened by Adm. Earl Mountbatten in 1955. In 1996, the decision was taken to move the *Daily Echo* to a new £35-million purpose-built centre at Newspaper House, Test Lane, Redbridge.

Following the move in 1997, the Above Bar Street building was then briefly occupied by Millets, the camping and outdoor clothing retail store, prior to its demolition in 1998. The main canopied postmodern entrance to the WestQuay Shopping Centre (seen here in 2007) now occupies this site. First published in 1888, the *Southern Daily Echo* is now owned by Newsquest (founded 1995), one of the country's largest publishers of local newspapers, which, in turn (since 1999), is owned by the US media group, Gannett.

This and next page: Although the Marlands Shopping Centre, built between Windsor Terrace and Portland Street on the site of the Hants and Dorset bus station (sold off following the 1986 bus privatisation), did not open until September 1991, it was still very much in the spirit of the 1980s. A previous attempt by Southampton City Council in 1982 to demolish the nineteenth-century Manchester Street terrace had been thwarted by environment secretary Michael Heseltine, but by 1988 the properties were boarded up and bulldozed, being deemed 'structurally unsound'. The Marlands was originally part of the Ronson family's Heron Property Development portfolio. With almost sixty store units, at the time of construction it was the largest of Southampton's new-style shopping malls. While its exterior (compared by one hostile critic to a 'Lego' construction) was unashamedly postmodern, the main atrium (seen here in two photographs taken *c.* 1991/92), with its glass roof, white walls, marble encased transparent lifts, fountain and the replicated two-storey former Manchester Street façade, was certainly most attractive. It was subsequently taken over by The Mall Corporation in 2004, and revamped in 2005/06, when the fountain was decommissioned due to healthy and safety issues. The Above Bar Street entrance (which followed that of the old, now defunct Manchester Street) was extensively redesigned and roofed over (again the original design can be seen here in the early 1990s photograph). The centre was rebranded as The Mall, but reverted to its former name again when it was sold in 2010 to The Other Retail Group for £136 million.

Despite its ups and downs, The Marlands has survived as, unlike Bargate or East Street, it gained a High Street presence from the additions of Poundland, F. Hinds, Savers, Costa Coffee, the Disney Store, Kodak Express, and latterly Starbucks coffee. The consequences of the loss, in 2014, of its flagship store Matalan (the unit being formerly occupied by Dunnes) remains to be seen.

Unfortunately, what Southampton gained in a shopping experience it lost out in any coordinated central bus terminus. The consequence for residents, students and visitors alike is one of confusion and chaos at the numerous bus stops scattered across a large area of the city centre. Public transport in Southampton, which has never really been that good, still remains something of a 'work in progress'.

Civic Centre, Guildhall Square & Commercial Road

Previous page: Begun in 1928 and completed in 1939, just before the start of the Second World War, the Civic Centre belongs to an era when civic buildings were unashamedly grand. By the 1960s, town halls and local government buildings had become bland and often unidentifiable, and often just another concrete and glass office block, as in the case of nearby Fareham's 1976 Civic Offices. The architect was Ernest Berry Webber (1896–1963), who specialised in the design of municipal buildings – both Dagenham and Hammersmith town halls were also by him. It was built in four stages – the foundation stone was laid by the Duke and Duchess of York, later King George VI and the Queen Mother, in 1930. The Municipal Block was opened in 1932; the Law Courts and 156-ft (47.6 metres) high Clock Tower in 1933; the Guildhall in 1937; and the 'Art Block' (art gallery, art school and library – the latter proposed retrospectively) in 1939, although this frontage was badly damaged by bombs in November 1940. Although a Grade II listed building since 1964, a number of alterations have been made since, notably in 1993 when the Central Library was completely (and very successfully) revamped and enlarged to incorporate three levels. The main Commercial Road entrance was remodelled back to the original appearance, after which a new foyer area and the very popular Fountains Café was created, which sadly closed in 2012. With the building of Marlands Shopping Centre and the widening of Civic Centre Road, the Rose Garden disappeared, and the fountain was relocated to its present location in front of the Art Gallery. The greatest alteration, however, has been to the west façade facing onto Havelock Road, when, in 2001, the Laws Courts moved to their new purpose-built location next to the old Ordnance Survey buildings in London Road. Then, in 2011, the police also moved (after five years of planning) to a larger, £32 million, purpose-built eight-storey central police station on the corner of Mountbatten Way and Southern Road. In 2010, work began on redeveloping both the old Law Courts and Central Police Station into the new maritime museum, SeaCity. It opened in 2012, and was designed by Wilkinson Eyre and built by contractor Kier Southern, with the help of £5 million from the Lottery Heritage Fund. Unfortunately, the rather grand Law Courts' entrance and steps, seen here in the late 1980s, has now been swept away, presumably in the name of ease of access.

Overleaf: This photograph, probably taken sometime in the early 1990s, is of the Tyrrell and Green department store at Nos 138–152 Above Bar Street. It is viewed from Guildhall Square, with the reflection of the Dutch-based C&A retail clothing store on the site opposite (where One Guildhall Square now is). This closed in 2001 when they pulled out of the UK after almost eighty years of trading. In 1897, Mr Reginald Tyrrell and Mr William Green opened their first shop together as 'drapers, milliners, ladies' and children's outfitters', but, since 1934, Tyrrell & Green had been part of the John Lewis Partnership. Designed by Yorke, Rosenberg & Mardall, this building was opened in 1956, with a third floor being added in 1958. A covered pedestrian passage led through into Park Walk. Although there was less then ten years between this building and its rival, Plummer's department store, opposite (opened in 1965; a distorted reflection of which can be seen in the windows on the left), the two were quite different. Tyrrell's always seemed rather dark and old-fashioned and almost 1930s-ish, with Plummer's more modern, with a delightful first-floor restaurant looking out across Guildhall Square. However, it was Plummer's that was to vanish, closing down in 1993, the building being taken over by the Southampton Institute of Higher Education (now Solent University) as a conference and teaching centre, and renamed the Sir James Matthews Building in 1994. The Tyrrell & Green name too vanished, becoming the same as that of parent company John Lewis, with the opening of WestQuay in September 2000. The huge store stood derelict and boarded up for another ten years, while plans for a new multi-million-pound 'arts complex' were proposed, threatened (in 2008 and again in 2010), then revitalised again. Eventually demolished in 2007, the site was grassed over, opening the planned vista between the Guildhall and East Park. Only now, in spring of 2014, has construction finally started for what is hoped will be the latest jewel in the so-called 'Cultural Quarter' crown.

This page and overleaf: Commercial Road stretches from Above Bar Street through to the junction of Nelson Gate. However, Southampton City Council's peculiar obsession with diverting one leg of crossroads has created an unnatural discontinuity at the junction with Havelock Road. The *Kelly's Street Directory* shows that, from 1865–1913, this side of the street was almost exclusively residential, and that only from 1921 onwards did it gradually become commercial, until 1939, when it was exclusively devoted to shops. The first four photographs record the delightful parade of restaurants (Nos 4–10) that once existed on the south side of Commercial Road from Havelock Road to the Mayflower Theatre, all of which were swept away in 1998. It was then that the La Margherita Italian restaurant, seen here, moved to its current location at Town Quay was constructed. Following the 1998 demolition, the site remained derelict and empty for the next fifteen years, blocked off with fence and billboards (lower picture on the next page), while various plans for 'Mayflower Plaza' seemingly came and went. In 2008, the latest proposal, the cost of which was estimated at £80 million, and now apparently named 'Mayflower Point', is comprised of 180 apartments with a seven-storey office and hotel. It was given the go-ahead, but failed to find sufficient office tenants. Fast-forward to 2012 and a new plan had been proposed and accepted instead, 'Mayflower Halls' – a £70 million project for the University of Southampton to build a three-block, fifteen-storey high 'vertical village'. It would accommodate 1,000 students, complete with gym, supermarket, 400 cycle racks and basement parking. In April 2014, during construction, there was an accidental fire on the roof of Block B. The new students' accommodation is currently scheduled to be completed by autumn 2014.

In 1928, the Empire Theatre opened, opposite the now redundant St Peter's church. Originally for the Moss Empire Group, it was designed by W. and T. R. Milburn, and built in the neo-Grecian style with a seating capacity of 2,356 (1,174 in the stalls), making it the largest theatre outside of London in the south of England. From 1933 onward it had a dual function as both a theatre and cinema, and the name changed to the Gaumont in 1950, by which time it was part of the Gaumont British Picture Corporation, later to be Rank. In 1982, with the decline in cinema attendances, Rank applied to convert it into a bingo hall, which (thankfully) was refused. It closed in 1986, reopening as the Mayflower Theatre the following year, after a £4-million reconstruction. It very successfully specialises in staging popular West End musicals and pantomimes, featuring well-known television actors and TV personalities, too numerous now to mention. More refurbishment followed in 2003 and 2012, enlarging the box office area and giving wheelchair access. The seating capacity is still given as 2,300, and it is now a Grade II listed building.

Brunswick Place, St Mary's Road

This and previous page: St Andrew's Presbyterian church, Brunswick Place, and the Lamb Memorial Hall (named after benefactor Andrew Lamb) extending along Dorset Street (since the 1960s part of the Inner Ring Road and the Charlotte Place roundabout), seen here not long before it was demolished in 1995. Built in 1853, it could seat up to 700, and was apparently known locally as the 'Scottish Church'. However, a combination of factors led to its decline and demise; firstly the large-scale demolition and clearance of much of the previous residential area between Dorset Street and St Mary's Road in the 1960s/70s, the construction of the Inner Ring Road (now the A33) and the huge Charlotte Place gyratory system. In 2005, the 270-bedroom Jury's Inn complex was built over the sunken car park, although it was still accessed from Compton Walk. Then, in 1972, the Congregational and Presbyterian Churches joined together to form the United Reform Church in England and Wales, the consequences of which was two URC churches quite close to each other (the other being the Congregational church in The Avenue, opposite Northlands Road, built in 1898). The final blow for St Andrew's came in the early 1980s, when it became apparent that £150,000 was needed to 'maintain structural safety', and the decision was made to combine the congregation with that of The Avenue church, which henceforth has become known as Avenue St Andrews URC. The older church was demolished in 1995 and replaced by a postmodern office block (seen here from Andrews Park) named Brunswick Gate, No. 23 Brunswick Place, and occupied by RBS and NatWest Customer Service Centre.

Next two pages: A story in four pictures of the Co-operative Society department store at Nos 60–64 St Mary's Road, thanks to photographs contributed by local historians Dave Goddard and Jim Brown. The Southampton Co-operative Society department store was built in 1934, apparently catering for 'drapery, outfitting, furnishing, funeral, boots … [with a] restaurant'. It was an elegant three-storey brick building, located between Crompton Walk (seen on the left in the first and third pictures) and the now long-since vanished Northam Street. The first photograph, from Dave Goddard, shows it still in its heyday. Judging from the cars, it is *c.* 1960s, with an imposing central entrance. Fast forward twenty years to October 1985 and my photograph (*below opposite*) illustrates that the terraced houses of Northam Street have already been cleared away (the empty open space being apparently used as a car park). Beyond that can now be seen the massive British Gas regional offices, opened in 1977. In the left foreground, the Co-operative Society department store is now derelict and boarded up, the ground-floor boarding covered with billboards and fly-posters, while the sign above reads: 'All Enquiries – Pearson's Commercial'. Sometime in the late 1980s, not long after my photograph, it was finally being demolished (see page 78, *top*). This act of needless, wanton civic vandalism was captured, this time by local historian and former Southampton police officer Jim Brown (*pictured overleaf, bottom*), almost from the same spot as the first picture (note that the former Halfway House pub is now renamed the Compton Arms). The roof and most of the interior has already gone, while there is scaffolding and crude fencing about what remains of the walls. Lastly, another of the author's photographs, taken a few years ago (*c.* 2011), but incredibly the view today (in 2014) is no different. Twenty-five years on, and the site is still empty and unused.

Compton Walk was once an ordinary street of terraced houses connecting St Mary's Road with East Park Terrace. Now it is a sad, truncated thoroughfare to the covered-in car park beneath Jury's Inn, and the smaller open-air car park behind The Edge (Southampton's largest and most popular gay nightclub since 1995) the former Halfway House (*c.* 1869) until 1974, reopened as the Compton Arms 1980–87, then named Aggie Greys. For a fascinating insight into how this area once looked, I would refer the reader to pages 94–104 of Jim Brown's *More Southampton Changing Faces.*

Dominating both the St Mary's and Southampton skyline since 1977 is the former British Gas building at Nos 78–80 St Mary's Road, when they moved their administration headquarters from Winchester. Since the late 1990s, however, the British Gas offices have been systemically converted into student accommodation for both Solent University and University of Southampton. It is now known as Orion's Point or Liberty Point, after the new tenants, Liberty Living plc. In 2012, this totalled 393 single study-bedrooms and thirty-eight self-contained studio apartments, spread through the twelve-storey Block A (west side, facing Dorset Street); the ten-storey Block B (east side, facing towards St Mary's); and the seven-storey Block C (fronting Charlotte Place, with a two-storey extension added in 2002). In 2012, British Gas announced their decision to cut 500 jobs from the call centre based at Dorset House, and this has prompted the possibility of yet more development for student accommodation. In its 2012 impact assessment, the council's city design manager describes how Block B 'presents a stark, dark and unwelcoming face to the north … for those approaching from The Avenue down Dorset Street'.

Northam Road & Six Dials

Today, Six Dials is just the name of a huge, bewildering, but comparatively short, dual carriageway that links Northam Road with the complex traffic light controlled junctions of Kingsway, New Road and the A33 south of Charlotte Place. The name is without meaning anymore. Only by looking at an old, early twentieth-century Ordnance Survey is it possible to understand how it got its name. New Road ran originally in a straight line east from East and Houndwell Parks, to be met by St Andrew's Road running at a 45 degrees angle, St Mary's Road angled in at 60 degrees, St Mark's Road coming from the Nichols Town district at 115°, Northam Road continuing east, still in a straight line (until it angled slightly at the junction of Brinton's Road and Derby Road towards the metal bridge over the railway), and finally – running dead straight south – St Mary's Street, with the Bridge Tavern public house on the corner.

In the 1930s, the main routes coming into Southampton from the east were, and still are, abysmal. The Woolston–Chapel floating bridge chain-ferry was only replaced in 1977 by the Itchen Toll Bridge, but even that has only two lanes, not wide enough for today's traffic. The Portsmouth Road is probably still no wider then it would have been in the 1930s. The 40 mph single carriageway, Thomas Lewis Way (the A335) also known as the Portswood bypass, was eventually opened in 1989, but this was originally planned to be a motorway link, the M272 (also known as the M27 Swaythling Link), directly connecting the M27 junction 5 to Central station, Mountbatten Way and the Western Docks. But what we have instead rather typifies the half-cock political indecisiveness and penny-pinching that Southampton still seems to have towards improving its road network, or, indeed, improving public transport as an alternative.

The other main east route, the A3024 Bursledon Road (and the A334 Townhill Park Road and Bitterne Road East from the M27 junction 7, which connect at Bitterne) also exemplify the same immediate post-war lost opportunities and failure of imagination. While the Northam Bridge over the Itchen dates from 1954, the Bitterne bypass was being talked about in the 1960s (it was eventually opened in 1982) but, in general, road widening on this crucial route continued to be done on a piecemeal basis. Apparently, even before the Second World War, Six Dials was something of a traffic bottleneck, when Southampton's first roundabout was established there in 1938. Because of the wooden barriers, it became known as the 'cattle market', but the trams could not negotiate the curve so the tracks went right through it, often followed at first by confused motorists. By 1960, plans were developed for a one-way gyratory system, and this was still in effect throughout the 1980s, only to eventually be completely swept away, along with much of the Victorian terraced houses and shops between Northam and Brinton's Road, in the period 1987–93.

Next page: All photographs of the redevelopment were taken in 1988. Seen top opposite are Nos 51–53 Northam Road, then the Glebe public house, formerly listed as a hotel, with the first publican from *c.* 1875. The one-way gyratory system is still in operation, with westbound traffic going up Northam Road on the left (looking towards New Road (and the grey 1970s Clifford House (offices and a ground-floor car showroom) in the distance. On the right is one-way eastbound Brinton's Road, the south side of which (Nos 1–49, up to St Mark's Road) having already been demolished. The taller building in the distance on the right is the Southampton Institute for Higher Education (until 1984 the Institute of Technology and Art) in East Park Terrace, since 2005 known as Solent University.

In the second picture, from 2011, what was once the Glebe, now sits in a truncated semi-pedestrian cul-de-sac, having had a succession of names in the late 1980s and 90s: the Queen Vic, the Goal House, the Victoria and, finally, in 2007, the King Alfred. Clifford House was subsequently demolished and replaced by a new, certainly more attractive, Premier Travel Inn, the design of which did at least make some belated concession to the once straight vista along Northam Road and New Road, since lost in the post-war road realignment. What had been Six Dials is now a thoroughly confusing traffic-light-controlled, multi-lane dual carriageway. Lit by arc lights, the main traffic is beyond the trees and metal barriers are on the right. Vehicular access into this part of Northam Road and St Mary's Street is through a traffic-light controlled junction with Brinton's Road and what had once been St Peter's Road, which, like much of St Mark's Road and St Mark's Terrace, has now disappeared.

By my calculation, this photograph shows Nos 14–4, on the north side of Brinton's Road, looking toward the junction (*see next page*) with Derby Road, as viewed from the already demolished south side. All of these properties were scheduled for demolition to make way for the new dual carriageway, as it carved its way north of Northam Road. Brinton's Road has now reverted to two-way traffic again, the first house number being No. 18, while opposite is open space and a small estate of new houses, built in the 1990s.

Another view of Brinton's Road on the north side looking west, with the junction of Derby Road on the right. The 'No Entry' signs show that this was still operating as the eastbound gyratory, with traffic feeding in from Trinity Road, while Derby Road (which still had the well-known 'reputation' it had first acquired in the 1960s as being at the heart of Southampton's 'red-light' district) was already blocked off. Vehicular access was presumably along Northbrook Road. The Glebe public house is just out of the picture to the left. The corner shop and adjacent workshop is No. 2 Brinton's Road; the terrace houses being demolished on the right are the odd numbers of Derby Road, Nos 1–9. The first houses now are Nos 11 and 16 respectively.

Another view of No. 2 Brinton's Road, looking east to the Derby Road junction, with the corner building on the right (covered in scaffolding) being No. 55 Northam Road.

A 'zoom in' close-up of No. 55 Northam Road, with the corner shopfront of No. 2 Brinton's Road on the left. This end of Derby Road is already fenced off, although the post box is still functioning.

Above: Another slight shift in viewpoint; this is Nos 55 to 63 Northam Road, the larger corner shop unit with the scaffolding being 'Savon Furniture & Carpets'. Just over a decade earlier, listed in the last (1975) *Kelly's Street Directory*, Nos 55–61 had been 'Nicolson's Marine Equipment – yacht chandlers'. On the right it is just possible to see the junction of Northumberland Road, and the Northam Road railway bridge.

Right: Looking along the east side (even numbers) of Derby Road, probably taken over the fencing behind the postbox (*seen on the picture opposite below*), the two-storey terraced houses, with steps and basement, await their fate. Again, everything here was about to be swept away.

Finally, on the left we see the corner of Northumberland Road and Nos 65, 65A, 67 and 69 Northam Road, the road already sloping towards the railway bridge, out of the picture, on the right. This area now is an empty, grassy wasteland, with the first three 'even' house numbers gone. On the odd side, almost everything up until Wolverston Road (Nos. 1-17) has vanished.

Northam Road (looking east towards the 1908 metal railway bridge), Derby Road (the rooftops on the left) and Northumberland Road, now completely severed from the main road and concealed behind wooden fencing, as seen in 2011. The ultimate consequence of all this upheaval and disruption is a brief, if rather confusing, three-lane dual carriageway, which then narrows back down to a bottleneck at the railway bridge, beyond which are the road junctions which now lead to the new 'Saints' football stadium. Traffic congestion still happens, but the two halves of St Mary's, once unified, are now divided by a tarmac wasteland, linked only by a series of rather uninviting subways and a traffic-light controlled pedestrian crossing at the junction of Brinton's Road. The two gasholders seen here are situated beyond the railway, actually in Britannia Road, and date from 1909 and 1935, this latter being the largest in Hampshire.

St Mary's Street from Kingsway, Marsh Lane & Three Field Lane

Another series of views, this time of the rear of the west side of St Mary's Street, as seen from Kingsway. This was prior to extensive redevelopment between 2000–04, which also saw the ancient (and in the 1990s, still vibrant) street market finally wither away, as the stalls shifted almost en masse to new locations in the precinct of Above Bar street and the now traffic-free space between Bargate and the junction of High Street and East Street. Southampton, like Portsmouth, its near-neighbour and rival, was always essentially working class, based as it was around its docks and manufacturing industry, with small farms and – until the 1950s – still mostly rural villages out on the fringe. Here there were more middle-class areas, larger houses, some even in their own grounds at Bitterne Park, or between Hill Lane and The Avenue, around Bassett Green and either side of Bassett Avenue. But, overall, its population is (or was) working- and lower-middle class, as reflected in the streets and architecture running down the west side of the Itchen River from Portswood, through St Mary's and Northam to Chapel. It would seem that successive town, and later city councils, throughout much of the twentieth century, have attempted to erode and eradicate these working-class communities, no doubt (as bureaucrats and town planners do) wishing impose order and modernity upon what they saw as unregulated lifestyles and haphazard chaotic development. Rather than work to improve the services and general appearance of these neighbourhoods, or empower their occupants to take control of their own environments, instead they prefer to swept everything away, often throwing the baby out with the bathwater. What bombs didn't achieve in the Second World War, eager planners and architects have continued to do since. Fortunately, so far, the inhabitants of this part of St Mary's have managed, despite all odds, to still retain something of that mixed, bustling, only semi-regulated diversity.

As viewed from Kingsway, a 'new' dual carriage planned to bypass St Mary's Street as long ago as 1950, but construction only began ten years later. This shows the rear of the former Bridge Tavern public house, perched on the very edge of the railway cutting where the Southampton–Waterloo line runs beneath St Mary's Street towards the 'gasworks bridge', with the now truncated North Front on the right. Originally, in 1830, the Red Rover, in the 1850s it was renamed the Bridge Tavern, its address being Nos 106–09 New Road. It was listed as a pub from 1871, with the local Portsmouth-based Brickwoods brewery from 1925, and later part of the Whitbread group from 1971, when Brickwoods (founded in 1848) was finally taken over. It closed as a pub in 1982 and at the time of this photograph was the Bridge Art Gallery. Its street façade (in the inset, the St Mary's Street frontage) is quite different, and – despite subsequent neglect and indifference – is still quite imposing. A new side road now leads from North Front to the new houses in Cavern Street.

Again viewed from Kingsway, looking down onto Cavern Street, before and after. Dating from the 1820s, Cavern Street, like Winton and Johnson Streets, originally ran in a straight line from St Mary's Street, almost as far as Palmerston Road. Although all three roads were still listed in the last pre-war *Kelly's* for 1936/37, by the beginning of the Second World War the old closely-packed terraces of workers' cottages fronting directly onto the street were already being demolished, and in 1950 the draft road layout for the new Kingsland Place was being drawn over the 1948 OS map, and following pretty much what was eventually built; a modest, but attractive, estate of low three- and four-storey flats and houses. Cavern Street was reduced to a short side road leading to rear car parking, although here there is still a pedestrian subway leading beneath the busy Kingsway to Craven Walk. Unfortunately, the redevelopment that saw Craven Street become residential again also caused the demise of the varied and interesting architecture fronting the west side of St Mary's Street itself, with everything between North Front and the corner of Johnson Street being swept away and the entire length replaced by a rather bland street façade.

The next truncated road, Winton Street, originally from 1820 until 1895 called Winchester Street, was, like Craven Street, part of the 'slum clearance' programmes in the late 1930s. At this time, it is used only for car parking for Kingsland Market. The last 1975 *Kelly's* gives a hint at the variety of trades in just this stretch from North Front to Johnston Street – four butchers, a cobblers, ladies hairdresser, a furniture store, an antique shop, a tobacconist, a grocer, sports outfitters, a drug store, a textile shop, two snack bars, a curry restaurant, a takeaway, a KFC and the North Star public house, dating from 1851 (closed briefly 1989–91 following a fire).

Continuing along the rear of St Mary's Street, the next (and final, before Kingsland Square) truncated side road is Johnson Street, on the corner of which (in the second picture, with the 'No Parking' sign on the back wall) was another public house. This dated from the 1840s, but is listed in *Kelly's* throughout much of the twentieth century as a 'beer retailer' until 1962, when it became Ye Dorsetshire Arms, and later, in the 1990s, the Clan of Scotland Club. Now the only surviving original building in this parade from North Front, in 2014 it is the Kingsland Foods and Halal Meat Store. Johnnie's Fisheries, on the opposite corner of Johnson Street, is now La Pescaderia, a 'Specialist Fishmonger'. Looming in the background is the 150-flat, sixteen-storey Albion Towers, in the Golden Grove estate, built in 1965 to the same design as Shirley Towers, over on the west side of the city. In 1996, following a petition submitted to the then MP, James Hill, the city council was fined £26,000 under the 1974 House & Safety at Work Act for exposing contractors and tenants to asbestos.

The final pre-redevelopment picture, still viewed from Kingsway, is to the south of Kingsland Square and the Plume of Feather public house. Again, everything seen here was demolished between 2000–04 and replaced by several ground-floor retail units (currently a hairdresser's and Best-One convenience store facing onto St Mary's Street), together with apartments and the regional headquarters for the Hyde Housing Group. This last building, with its different window shapes, ground-floor arch window and slightly protruding street façade, is the most attractive of the entire modern rebuild. Some commercial units and light industry still operate in this locality between Kingsway and St Mary's Street, but from Harrison's Cut and Chapel Street, towards Cook Street, is mostly student accommodation for City College. Since 1952, this has gradually expanded upwards and outwards from the old 1866 Victorian workhouse building next to St Mary's parish church, changing its name from Southampton Technical College in 1995.

A view of the junction of Threefield Lane and Marsh Lane from the corner of Evan Street and Houndwell Place, with the pedestrian entrance to the East Street Centre on the right beneath the concrete canopy of the rooftop car park, *c.* 1987/88. On the extreme left is Central Hall, opened in 1925 and built by Joseph Rank for the Methodist Church, the architect being the Mancunian Arthur Brocklehurst. It was a venue used by a number of evangelical preachers, including a young Billy Graham, not long after the Second World War. In 1965, it was sold to Hampshire County Council Education Services, and became an annex to nearby City College, until it was subsequently purchased in 1989 by the Community Church (a Christian evangelical movement founded in the early 1970s). From 2007 onward, it was known as the New Community Church, part of the Pioneer network of missionary churches. It has a seating capacity of 800. Looming behind the dome of Central Hall is the fourteen-storey Dukes Keep, built in 1976 and comprising of 66,800 sq. ft of office space. Despite a renovation in 2008, it is seemingly still struggling to find full tenancy.

Looking down Threefield Lane it is possible to see the structural framework taking shape for the three-storey Wessex House (occupied on a twenty-five year-lease since 1988 by Ernst & Young, accountants). Beyond that is the slightly smaller 'sister' office block, Threefield House (similarly occupied by Jardine insurance brokers). Immediately behind this looms Richmond House (which we saw earlier, viewed from Terminus Terrace), while on the right is the rather depressing brutalist pedestrian entrance, under the concrete canopy of the rooftop car park, to the 1975 East Street Centre. The road in the foreground (raised up in a hump to allow a pedestrian subway across to Central Hall) is actually Evan Street as it becomes Marsh Lane. Looking at the Alan Godfrey reproduction Ordnance Survey map (Southampton East, 1910), the original Evan Street, which dated from the eighteenth century and was known as York Street during the nineteenth century, originally ran south from Houndwell Place to a sort of X-shaped junction with East Street, Marsh Lane and the old St Mary's Street. The older houses were demolished in the 1930s, and the 1950 plan envisaged the current, much shorter Evens Street being widened and angled eastward to configure with St Mary's Place.

The end of another era, 2013/14, with the demolition of the East Street Centre, viewed here from Marsh Lane. Opened in 1975, and at one time branded as EaSTreet, it was Southampton's first (and least successful) shopping centre. It was very much in the 1970s style, with concrete and glass, a rooftop car park, a modern corner pub – the Royal Oak (apparently popular with students at City College, just five minutes walk away) – and the monstrous, thirteen-storey, grey, concrete office block, Capital House, No. 1 Houndwell Place. This building is distinguished by its open, external concrete spiral fire escape stairwell on its southern side. East Street had once directly connected the High Street with St Mary's Street, with the front façade and dome of Central Hall visible at the end, but this vista was blocked off by the new shopping centre. The Debenhams department store was a more traditional, late Victorian/Edwardian Queen's Buildings destroyed in the Second World War, rebuilt and enlarged in the 1950s/60s, but still known as Edwin Jones until 1973. Despite Debenhams being nearby (Edwin Jones until 1973; the late Victorian/ Edwardian Queen buildings were destroyed in the Second World War and were rebuilt in the 1950s/60s), the commerical centre of gravity moved away from East Street, and – with the eventual demise in the late 1980s and early 1990s of its key 'flagship' stores: Comet Electrical, Courts Furniture and Tandy Electronics – even the false gaiety of bright blue-and-yellow paint failed to attract customers. The upper floor died first, until it too, rather like the Bargate Centre, became little more then a rather dingy, depressing pedestrian thoroughfare, as one hurried to or from the Evans Street/Marsh Lane subway (with its 'New York City-style' graffiti) or the walkway leading between the concrete front entrance pillars of Capital House and the two-storey Royal Oak (itself nestled under the concrete car park roof) and out into the green space of Houndwell Park opposite.

Finally, in 2012, it was closed, and plans were submitted by Arcadian Estates Development for a new £32-million, 60,000 square feet (5,574 square metres) Morrisons superstore to be built there instead; demolition started in late 2013, with a completion date projected for the end of 2014 or early 2015. The Royal Oak public house and an 'enhanced' Capital House will survive, but now both free-standing and with a landscaped pedestrian area connecting East Street, St George's Street (right now nothing more then a service yard for Debenhams) and Evans Street, where the subway too is already closed off, to be replaced by a surface-level crossing, which will hopefully bring the ground-floor main entrance of Central Hall back into view again.

Acknowledgements

Southampton is blessed with a multitude of excellent 'past & present' style photography books, but I would particularly like to single out local historian and author, Jim Brown's, *Southampton's Changing Faces* (Breedon Books, 2005) and his follow-up, *More Southampton Changing Faces* (Breedon Books, 2008). Both contain some remarkable photos of Southampton as it once was. Likewise, Tony Gallaher's *Southampton Since 1945* (originally by Sutton Publishing, 1998) gives very interesting 'snapshots' of views in the late 1940s/early 50s, again comparing to the contemporary, with some of the images included in this book. For same delightful aerial images of Town Quay and the Eastern Docks (especially in the 1960s and 70s), I would recommend David L. William's *Docks and Ports: Southampton* (Ian Allen, 1984). As always, the Alan Godfrey Ordnance Survey maps are both informative and a wonderful record of the past. For Southampton there are three maps: Southampton (West); Southampton (East) and Southampton Docks – all 1908 to 1910. From my own collection there is *The Illustrated Guide to Southampton*, an illustrated A–Z compiled by Ian Broad in 1982, and *Southampton Remembered* by Maureen Burness (Milestone Publications, 1985). I have also referred to, and quoted fragments from, the city planning department's brochure, *Lower Town & Quayside Strategy*, from 1985. I also have a copy of the city council's *City Waterfront* brochure, probably published *c.* 1988, as well as the two *Above Bar Redevelopment* brochures, also from 1988. These include the draft proposals to roof over Guildhall Square and the top end of Above Bar Street.

On a more personal level, I would like to thank Jim Brown, in particular, for his response to my initial request for information in the *Daily Echo*. Jim has compiled a number of excellent books of Victorian, Edwardian and early twentieth-century Southampton, including those mentioned above, which are well worth reading. Jim also contributed his own photograph of the Co-operative Department Store in St Mary's Road, in the process of being demolished, together with another picture of it in its heyday from his colleague, Dave Goddard; my thanks and appreciation to them both. A word too for another of Jim Brown's colleagues, Dave Marden, who attempted to help identify several 'mystery' photos, believed to be somewhere in the Eastern Dock. Unfortunately, given that I have not been able to confidently confirm the exact locations, I have omitted them from this collection. My thanks also to Mr Richard Cutler, the current Honorary Consul of the Federal Republic of Germany, and especially to his predecessor, Mr Roger Thornton, who sent me a detailed, two-page email, giving a brief history of the sixty-year connection that had existed between the German Consulate in Southampton and Wainwright & Bros & Co., up until quite recently. I would also like to thank Anna Welsh, city council customer support, and especially Maria Newbery, curator of maritime and local history, in her attempts – unfortunately so far fruitless – to locate the Ocean Village model; and Colin Williams, of Williams Shipping, for helping indentify two barges at Town Quay where the company used to be based. I would also like to thank the helpful staff at the Civic Centre reference library.

All photographs were taken by, and are the property of, the author, unless stated otherwise in the text. All opinion and comments expressed, and any unintentional errors within the text, are entirely those of the author.